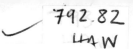

Creating Through
DANCE

CREATING THROUGH
DANCE
REVISED EDITION

ALMA M. HAWKINS
With a New Introduction
by Charlotte Irey, University of Colorado

A DANCE HORIZONS BOOK
Princeton Book Company, Publishers
Princeton, New Jersey

A Dance Horizons Book
Princeton Book Company, Publishers
POB 57
Pennington, NJ 08534

ISBN 0-916622-65-7 (hardbound edition)
ISBN 0-916622-66-5 (paperbound edition)
LC # 87–63489

Cover photograph: "Fractional Assemblies"
performed by Ronald Brown and Angelica Leung
of the UCLA Dance Company, 1987. Photograph
by Becky Villaseñor.

The photographs in this book are used by
permission of the UCLA Dance Department.

Introduction

There are new books and then there are books which remain always new because they focus on concepts. *Creating Through Dance* by Alma M. Hawkins is such a book. It is why I always keep it close at hand. It is there to remind me that providing excellent technical training for students is not enough. Providing them with an opportunity to experience dance as a creative art and thereby develop their creative potential is paramount.

This would be an excellent textbook for a college course in methods of teaching dance, as well as an important reference for a graduate seminar. It is because this book can be used at so many levels that it is such a valuable book to have in your library.

For the less experienced dancer, it leads the way to exploration of self, the development of a meaningful vocabulary, and the basic principles of choreography. For the less experienced teacher, this book serves as a directional map for guiding students through various stages of training and creative development. It is not a "how to" book. Instead, it reminds one that a sound dance education is based on principles and concepts, and to share one's own dance experience with students demands careful preparation. It emphasizes the responsibility of the teacher as facilitator and critic. It deals with the difficult problem of grading and evaluating student works. For the experienced teacher, who sometimes gets side-tracked in the mundane rituals of academia, the book provides a route back to the principles of the art of dance which excited one in the first place. It serves as a reminder of what teaching dance is all about. I have consistently referred to this book in my teaching. One only has to view my copy to know that it has been well used.

The reprinting of this very valuable book will be welcomed by all of us in higher education. I know it will be used and valued. It is very, very important that the writings of Dr. Hawkins, such a significant figure in the development of dance in higher education, be preserved.

Charlotte York Irey
Director of Dance
University of Colorado at Boulder

Preface

This book has been written with the belief that those of us interested in creative dance have an obligation to give serious attention to the art of movement as a *whole*. For far too long we have been inclined to view dance narrowly and incompletely, in terms of isolated component parts. Our interest in good technical performance has caused us to emphasize movement and to neglect creativity. We are constantly tempted to give value to technique as an end in itself rather than as a means to an end.

Comparatively little thought and time have been given to the phenomenon of creativity and its relationship to the study of choreography. We have been uncertain about the relationship between the creative aspects of dance and the development of the dance instrument. This uncertainty has caused some to overlook creativity as an aspect of the dancer's development.

Today there is increased interest in dance as a creative experience. Concepts about the teaching-learning process are taking a more definite shape. People are becoming more sophisticated in their understanding of dance, and the art of movement seems to be maturing.

The development of creativity in dance has long been a major concern to me. Through study and teaching experiences I have sought to understand the creative nature of dance and the implications for teaching. In this book I have discussed the concepts that I consider fundamental to the understanding of dance as a creative experience.

Because I believe that all aspects of dance must be presented in relation to the ultimate creative goal, I have tried to present an overview of the total experience. Many phases of the discussion, therefore, are necessarily brief. However, if I have succeeded in contributing to the idea that the vital and persisting core of dance is creativity and that every aspect of the dance experience has a significant relationship to creative development of the individual, then I will have achieved my primary purpose.

Acknowledgment is due to Mr. Nik Krevitsky for the illustrations which appear in this book.

A.M.H.

Contents

"Porcelian Dialogues" by Murray Louis performed by the UCLA Dance Company, 1987.
Photograph by Becky Villaseñor.

one

Dance as a creative experience

Dance is one of man's oldest and most basic means of expression. Through the body, man senses and perceives the tensions and rhythms of the universe around him, and then, using the body as an instrument, he expresses his feeling responses to the universe. From the fabric of his perceptions and feelings he creates his dance. Through his dance he relates to his fellow man and to his world.

Man's basic impulse to communicate through movement is set in action by motivations that are sometimes purely social, and other times essentially expressive, in nature. Dance resulting from either type of motivation is a unifying experience for the human being. As a social group activity, dance acts as a force that integrates or binds together. Through rhythmic movement the individual relates to others in a socially satisfying manner. As an expressive activity, dance enables the individual to relate to his environment in a highly personal and unique fashion. Through this expressive experience, which entails sensing, clarifying, and stating self, dance gives the creator a feeling of self-integration and harmonious relationships with his world. Both kinds of dance experiences are significant—the experience which arises from social drive, and that which results from man's need to discover and give tangible form to the aesthetic aspects of his encounter with life.

It is the expressive motivation, however, that leads to the development

3

of dance as an art. Dance as a work of art may be described as the expression of man's inner feelings transformed by imagination and given form through the medium of movement. The dance is a symbolic form which reveals the creator's inner vision. A dance, when presented as an art object, becomes an aesthetic experience for observers to perceive and share.

PERCEPTION OF MOVEMENT

As a work of art, dance has an inherent communicative power. This is so because human movement, the material of dance, is the essence of life. It grows out of life, reflects life, and is life. Therefore it is not surprising that movement is readily perceived and understood.

We use movement in our daily lives as a fundamental means of communication. For example, we respond to a question with a nod of the head or a shrug of the shoulder. Human feelings are revealed through such movements as the joyous jumping and clapping of the child or the tightly contracted and rocking torso of the grieved one. Spontaneous gestures such as these convey felt meanings and often speak more strongly than words.

We use movement as a means of experiencing and knowing. For example, basic concepts and symbols such as those related to shapes—round and square, time duration—long and short, distances—near and far, and weights—light and heavy, are learned through movement exploration and the neuromuscular sensing mechanism.

This kind of perceiving is made possible by man's innate capacity for inner mimicry and empathy with movement and movement tensions. The kinesthetic sense, made possible by an intricate network of nerves and muscles, enables the human being to "feel into" and perceive the movement gestures of his fellow man. This sensitive mechanism, which allows man to empathize with everyday gestures, also allows him to perceive dance as an art experience.

Man has the innate capacity to perceive and comprehend movement used as simple gesture and as art. Those people who find dance difficult to understand do so because their responding mechanism has become dulled from lack of use. A gap that seems insurmountable exists between the everyday use of movement for expressive purposes and the more abstracted use of movement in dance. Understanding, then, is a matter of experience.

Dance as a communicative art uses movement as its material, but the movement in dance is different from the everyday gesture in that it is distorted or removed from the natural and transformed into art. The creator strives to capture the essence of a particular sensory experience, and then, through a fresh and imaginative use of movement, he choreographs a dance that will evoke a feeling response. Only as the movement is abstracted and removed from its everyday form is the perceiver able to experience the illusion created by the work. The experienced choreographer knows well that the magic of a highly abstracted work can be destroyed by the sudden appearance of a movement pattern that is closely associated with the everyday world. As the illusion is lost the experience becomes personal rather than aesthetic.

Choreographing means more than assembling movements. The artist is concerned with what results from the organization of movement rather than with the mere arrangement. As a craftsman the dancer may construct a sequence of movements, but as an artist he creates an organic entity. Constructing and creating are two quite different processes, as we shall see. From an inner impulse comes the first movement of the dance. From this impulse and sustained emotional power evolves a continuum of movement, which projects the image of the creator. The completed dance assumes a form that has unity and gives the illusion of "aliveness." It is this quality of aliveness that stimulates the observer to perceive the dance as a happening, as something coming into being.

To achieve this aliveness, the choreographer must manipulate and organize his material so that it becomes an integrated whole, a nonverbal Gestalt. As the dance unfolds something new emerges. The finished work acts as a symbol which, in turn, causes feeling responses and thus reveals the creator's image, his dreams, and his vision of life. The challenge is to transform the movement material and design the form in such a way that the final dance becomes an exquisite abstraction of human experience which possesses such clarity and unity that the work is readily perceived as a meaningful and aesthetically satisfying experience.

The magic and communicative power of a dance, then, emerges through the unfolding of a simple, unified form rather than through the perception of isolated elements or gestures. The flow of energy and resultant forces perceived in designed relationships create the illusion. Therefore, the dancer's awareness of the relationship between form and expression is the factor that distinguishes the true dance that is a work of art from the so-called dance that is really nothing more than an ordinary event. The so-called dance is constructed of isolated and meaningless meanderings that fail to evoke any aesthetic response. Dance, as a work of art, is organized and achieves a form that is capable of involving the spectator with the opening movement and sustaining his attention to the end.

The task of the dancer as artist is to mold movement in such a way that it becomes an articulated form with the power to create the desired illusion and convey the essence of human experience. The movement is removed from the world of actuality and transformed so that the inherent force relationships create a world of magic and, at the same time, evoke felt meanings that are associated with life experiences. In this way the artist's image is given an external form that may be perceived as an aesthetic object and understood in terms of human experience.

MAN'S IMPULSE TO CREATE

Why does man create? Why does he make art objects? Undoubtedly he does so because of a basic drive that causes the human being to react to and become a part of the great adventure of life. This drive to know, to relate, and to become is an aspect of human nature that appears to transcend the basic preservation needs and the search for material satisfactions.

Man's innate curiosity and urge toward discovery are believed to be deeply imbedded in human nature. Murphy, the noted psychologist, tells us that there are

> ... deep forces within that strive fundamentally for the gratification of the need to understand; forces resistant to standardization and the molding process; forces that nervously and restlessly cut through the chrysallis of culture.[1]

The impulse toward creativity and aesthetic experiences is fed by the inner spirit that urges man to move forward and upward. Related to the creative impulse are basic sensory needs that cause man to seek experiences that are rich in color, tone, and rhythm. He uses these sensory experiences as a means of perceiving his surroundings and orienting himself to his world. Perhaps, as Murphy says,

> ... The potentials for becoming a human being, as compared with the less complex kind of animal, lie largely in this enrichment and elaboration of the sensory and motor ranges of experience and the life of symbolism which depends on this life.[2]

The explanation of man's creativeness, according to authorities, is to be found in the understanding of human nature. Apparently it is as much a part of nature to seek aesthetic experiences, to be curious, to discover, to imagine, and to stretch for new understandings as it is to

---

[1] Gardner Murphy, *Human Potentialities* (New York: Basic Books, Inc., 1958), p. 18.
[2] Murphy, *Human Potentialities*, p. 18.

perpetuate the basic biologic functions and the cultural heritage of man. The creative impulse appears to play a vital role in perceptual clarification and expression of felt meanings, both of which are significantly related to the process of self-actualization.

Although the need to create cannot be explained as readily as other needs, it is just as real as the need for food, shelter, and love. The spirit, the values, and the dreams of mankind are more abstract necessities, but are no less essential than physical necessities to the full development of the human being. Man seeks creative and aesthetic experiences because they enrich him as a person, help him become an integrated individual, and help him feel in harmony with his world. Rogers says that man's tendency to actualize himself, to become his potentiality, appears to be the mainspring of creativity.[3]

The fundamental ingredient in dance is the impulse to create. The urge to sense, discover, and relate tends to culminate in the creative act. The dancer, during the process of creating, needs to explore his sensory world, his cognitive world, and his affective world. From this searching encounter emerges a unique expression in the form of a dance. This act of creating a unified art object gives the creator a new sense of integration and wholeness.

VALUE OF CREATIVE EXPERIENCE

In this day of ever-expanding technological developments that place greater and greater emphasis on specialization, the human being needs experiences that aid him in achieving a feeling of wholeness. In the midst of a trend toward specialization and segmentation, he must find adequate sources of communicating with his fellow man—communicating and sharing that result in a sense of unity and belonging. Today, as never before, educators must be concerned with helping the student better understand himself and his world. Each individual should have opportunity for experiences that will assist him in becoming an integrated personality capable of relating to others and to his environment.

Even though we know that the human being must have a sense of adequacy and uniqueness to function effectively, our current cultural values are such that the individual is encouraged to conform rather than transform. He is urged to reflect and re-produce rather than to create.

---

[3] Carl R. Rogers, "Toward a Theory of Creativity," in *Creativity and Its Cultivation*, ed. Harold H. Anderson (New York: Harper & Row, Publishers, 1959), p. 72. © 1959 by Harper & Row, Publishers. Reprinted by permission of the publishers.

He is encouraged to take in and receive rather than to give out and contribute. All too seldom is he motivated to discover and express himself in terms of his uniqueness. Such pressures for conformity tend to be a disintegrating factor that stifles the potential development of the individual as a unique personality. The involvement of students in meaningful experiences that provide a counterbalance for the high value now placed on technology, mechanization, and materialism is the challenge of our day. Surely an essential part of the educator's task is to develop people who are creative and have confidence in themselves as individuals of worth and integrity.

It is in this area of human experience that dance and the other creative arts make a significant contribution. The basic urge to create is ever present. Our task is one of releasing and nourishing the impulse so that each individual has the opportunity to enjoy and benefit from that which is rightfully his possession—the power to create.

DANCER AS CREATOR

The mature creative power of the dancer emerges as a result of meaningful experiences. It does not "just happen," nor does it appear as a result of an accumulation of various isolated experiences. Instead it unfolds and evolves as a person discovers dance, sees the differentiated aspects in relation to the whole, and comes to know dance as a creative process through which he states himself with increasing confidence and clarity.

Since the value of the creative experience resides in its very nature and process, the individual who sets out to study dance should experience it from beginning to end as a creative activity. The heart of the experience is creativity and the expressive communicative aspects of dance. Movement is studied as the material of dance. Movement skills as well as all aspects of dance study are understood as a means and not an end in themselves. The primary goal is the experiencing of dance as a creative art. Therefore each aspect of the dance study is experienced in relation to another aspect and, in context, as a whole. Only as the various experiences are seen in their true relationship will they foster the release and the development of the dancer's potential creative power.

In the following chapters we will consider the dance experience in some detail. What is involved? What are the significant aspects or ingredients of dance as a creative art? Of course it is impossible to single out any one facet for discussion without being aware of its interdependence with other aspects. No aspect exists in isolation. But for purposes of clarification, it seems desirable that selected phases of the experience be examined occasionally in the hope that such a study will further the understanding of interrelationships and of the dance experience as a whole.

We begin with an explanation of the core of the dance experience, which is developing creativity. This explanation is followed by discussions of increasing aesthetic awareness, moving with control, creating with form, evaluating the product, and, finally, designing the total creative experience.

Alwin Nikolais leads a workshop as part of the Regent's Lecture Series in Dance at UCLA, 1982. Photograph by Spencer Snyder.

two

Developing creativity

NATURE OF CREATIVITY

Creativity is the heart of dance. It is the basic phenomenon in the act of making a dance and, also, in the perceiving of the finished work. Because man is endowed with a unique ability to create, he is able to bring into being ideas, symbols, and objects. The arts emerge because of man's desire to probe for fresh, penetrating views of his life experiences and because of his desire to give outward form to his unique and imaginative response. It is these urges that cause the dancer to choreograph.

The French novelist Malraux says that creating means seeing, reducing, and ordering. According to him the creator surrenders to his world of experience, takes possession and control of that which he sees, and brings about a reduction and a metamorphosis that results in an entity that is unified and unique.[1]

Erich Fromm, psychoanalyst and philosopher, believes that it is the "creative attitude" that makes it possible for the individual to see and

---

[1] André Malraux, *The Voices of Silence* (New York: Doubleday & Company, Inc., 1953), pp. 274-76.

respond creatively.[2] He does not mean "seeing" in the usual sense, which motivates an act of cognition and verbalization—in other words, a mental act. Seeing, as he interprets it, involves experiencing and perceiving by the whole person with a high degree of inner and outer awareness. This seeing is more than recognizing and reporting.

Although the exact nature of the creative process is still mysterious, there is considerable agreement about certain characteristics of the act. We know that the creative process involves a taking in of sensory data, a feeling about that which is perceived, an exploration of percepts and feelings, an imaginative relating of present and stored experiences, feelings, and meanings, and finally the forming of a new product.

Irving Taylor and other psychologists believe that the creative process consists of four basic stages, which may be identified as the periods of exposure, incubation, illumination, and execution.[3] Jenkins, a philosopher, who refers to these phases of the creative act as stages of seeing and appreciating, refining and expressing, and forming, believes that the various phases of the aesthetic process do not exist as isolated stages of behavior and that they do not happen in a sequential fashion. Instead the process follows a pattern of development that is cyclical rather than linear. He says that

> . . . Creation, as the culmination of this process, is most exactly conceived as vibrating between two poles, or as facing in two directions. It looks backward toward its source, seeking to attain a clearer apprehension of the particularity it is dealing with. At the same time, it looks forward toward its product, seeking through this to make its vision more articulate and permanent. These two phases can be described as internalization and externalization, or as insight and embodiment, or as contemplation and concretion. The important point is that these are phases in a cycle that is cohesive and recurrent.[4]

The various phases of the creative act are interwoven and fused in such a way that the vision of the artist is made concrete, and a single entity is produced. Anyone who has observed creative people at work knows that each artist must work through the process in his own way. There is no chartered path that leads to the final product. As Zilboorg has said, an artist's idea is a free-floating thing. He feels the necessity to draw a building and, for some reason, sees colors and various shapes.

---

[2] Erich Fromm, "The Creative Attitude," in *Creativity and Its Cultivation*, ed. Harold H. Anderson (New York: Harper & Row, Publishers, 1959), pp. 44, 45. © 1959 by Harper & Row, Publishers. Reprinted by permission of the publishers.

[3] Irving A. Taylor, "The Nature of the Creative Process," in *Creativity*, ed. Paul Smith (New York: Hastings House, Publishers, Inc., 1959), pp. 61-66.

[4] Iredell Jenkins, *Art and the Human Enterprise* (Cambridge, Mass.: Harvard University Press, 1958), p. 117.

Finally his vision becomes objectified as a building. In a free-floating fashion he searches involuntarily until he becomes aware of what happens, his will gets hold of it, and he reproduces what he has to produce.[5]

The following account of a young choreographer's experience during the creative process is interesting and illustrates something of the erratic nature of this act:

> In choreographing "Fantasies" to Webern's *Five Pieces for String Quartet*, the spark of the idea was originally produced by the movement that had been choreographed for the themes in the first musical section. The whole movement pattern seemed to be permeated with breath and a state of dance tension associated by me with a dream state, or an awareness of the fantasy-like states of mind that fill the self with imagined beauty. Perhaps it was the realization that dreams were man's first awesome proof that he is spirit as well as flesh, that influenced my own attitude toward dance.
>
> Some would say that this dream state is an escape from awareness of the realities of everyday life. If it be an escape then it still reflects those same pieces and bits of reality that have inspired the self to envision a feeling about living.
>
> The first conscious awareness of what I was trying to express came after the idea was transformed into movement. Once the right movement state was found and selected, I used it as my standard of value for organization and selection of the rest of the movement.
>
> After finishing the first musical section, I began the "Sea Scene," which followed in what seemed like a logical sequence. But my mind had jumped ahead to the second musical section, which was a development of the original scene. I kept seeing images of the whole development. Because I couldn't force the first silence in the music to be something it didn't want to be, I dropped the section and worked on the second quartet. As I reflect back on the experience, I find that this section was the most satisfying. I was working at home. My mind was struggling with the problem of form and how to actualize the image. After approximately five minutes, I began writing down the whole section while it poured out from beginning to end. This was the only section that wasn't changed when I worked it out with the cast.
>
> Now my mind was free and I felt no conflict. The "Sea Scene" found its own expression shortly after. I felt wonderful because the first three sections satisfied me to some extent.
>
> Time was my enemy and I finally made myself choreograph the last musical section because I knew that the dance would suffer if I ignored this practical realization. This section was picked apart, rearranged, and finally set to give a general idea of the intention that I had. But the excitement and rightness of it didn't compare to the second quartet. Then hurriedly I gave a vague impression of the second silence in the music which I wanted to be the quality of weightlessness and complete negation of gravity. This section, which I called the "orbital section," suffered most of all.
>
> There were moments of great pleasure experienced while I was making this dance. I recall the unfolding mental image of the second quartet; the

[5] Gregory Zilboorg, "The Psychology of the Creative Personality," in *Creativity*, ed. Smith, p. 28.

pleasure of moving through the fantasy scene; the "almost" ending fall sensation; the complimentary feeling tones of the music, set, lights, and costumes; and the pleasure of enjoying the individual interpretations of the dancers. The joy in making any dance comes from creating the form which expresses certain impressions of life felt mostly by the individual.[6]

The person who sets out to create a dance or any other work of art does so because of a persistent urge to pursue an idea or feeling. The creator has the sense of being pulled toward an unknown or partially envisioned end product. Some experience with sensory data has resulted in a stimulus or motivation that calls for creative action. Sometimes the motivation that seems compelling may turn out to be tentative and is pushed aside by other experiences. But some motivations do endure and demand resolution. All results of the creative effort are not equally successful. The degree to which the final product is successful depends on many factors.

FACTORS AFFECTING CREATIVITY

Although all human beings have some capacity for creativity, the degree and quality of achievement may not be the same for all persons. The final creative act will be influenced by internal and external factors, such as personality characteristics and individual experience. Recent research in the field of creativity suggests that highly creative people possess certain common personality characteristics. These characteristics can be identified as the capacity to be puzzled; "openness" to new experiences; aesthetic sensitivity; cognitive flexibility; high-level creative energy; and imagination. It may be that the amount and quality of creative output is influenced by the degree to which one possesses these characteristics.

Even if we were sure that such characteristics as those mentioned are significant factors, there still remains the question of how much such behavior patterns can be modified through experience. We do know that those who are to grow creatively must have experiences that stimulate and encourage the process of perceiving, feeling, imagining, and expressing. They must learn to see not the mere shape but the whole entity with all its differentiated aspects and interrelationships, to feel deeply and find delight in the simplest elements, to respond sensitively and imaginatively, and to express unique feeling and ideas with clarity and confidence.

---

[6] Statement made by Karin Waid, senior in Dance, May 1962, UCLA.

Conditions necessary for creativity

Creative growth flourishes best in an environment that allows the individual to discover and to explore his unique responses, and the impulse toward creativity must be nurtured in a special way. The task of facilitating the release and development in creativity is somewhat similar to the problem of getting a small, frightened animal to come out of a deep hole. You cannot demand or get behind it and push. Instead you must tempt, attract, and reassure. Neither can the creator be prodded or pushed. Not until he feels safe and secure will he edge his way into creative experiences, dare to think for himself, see in his own way, and make his unique response. Creativity develops as the self is ready to create. Those who are interested in helping individuals develop creativity must be concerned with environmental conditions that foster this kind of growth.

According to Rogers, those who want to facilitate creativity must know how to establish external conditions that will nourish the internal condition necessary for the emergence of creativity. Certain conditions seem to have a positive effect, whereas other conditions have a negative effect.[7] Rogers, and others who have studied this aspect of behavior, believe that psychological safety and freedom are two of the most basic conditions needed for creativity.

Psychological safety evolves from a working situation in which the emphasis is on acceptance and understanding of the individual with a minimum of external evaluation. In the dance situation this means that the student needs to feel that the teacher accepts him as an individual of unconditional worth and has faith in him and in his creative ability. He needs to know that his creative effort will be respected even when the results do not reach the desired goal. He needs to be reassured about certain aspects of his work that are successful. Whenever the facilitating person provides this kind of a learning climate, he is fostering creativity.

The dance student should have opportunities to share his work with the group. Just as other students display their paintings and read their poems, the dancer should show his choreography. It is through performing and sharing his work that he is able to overcome his feeling of isolation and increase his sense of belonging. As the student becomes convinced about the sincerity and respect that surrounds him and his work, he will find it possible to relax and be more daring, as well as to work without making excuses or putting up defenses. As he senses this

---

[7] Carl R. Rogers, "Toward a Theory of Creativity," in *Creativity and Its Cultivation*, ed. Anderson, pp. 78-80.

respect of others, he finds it easier to accept himself and to feel pride in his work. This kind of acceptance leads to a new confidence and enthusiasm for creative activity in dance.

The feeling of psychological safety is enhanced by the capacity of the facilitating person to understand and respond emphatically. True acceptance implies more than a superficial gesture. For example, Rogers says,

> If I say that I "accept" you, but know nothing of you, this is a shallow acceptance indeed, and you realize it may change if I actually come to know you. But if I understand you, empathetically, see you and what you are feeling and doing from your point of view, enter your private world and see it as it appears to you, and still accept you, then this is safety indeed. In this climate you can permit your real self to emerge, and to express itself in varied and novel formings as it relates itself to the world. This is a basic fostering of creativity.[8]

This kind of feeling relationship encourages the creator to confront experiences with an "openness." It helps him to become task oriented and less concerned about his personal status and security. In this type of climate something that might be called "trust in the teacher" seems to emerge. The learner becomes more willing to venture into new depths because he has faith that the teacher will not place him in a situation that he cannot handle.

The nature and amount of external evaluation is also a factor that affects the creative climate and feeling of psychological safety. The emphasis in the creative situation should be on internal evaluation or self-evaluation. To know that the ends are not fixed and that one's work will be accepted on its own merit is enormously freeing. The absence of external standards that are used as measuring sticks leaves the individual free to experiment with his ideas and to work in his own way. This does not mean that students do not work towards excellence, nor that there is an absence of sharing of ideas about that which is creative. It does imply that observers do not make judgments in terms of right and wrong or good and bad. This kind of measurement necessitates the use of predetermined standards that are stifling and undesirable.

Creative growth will take place more readily in an atmosphere where the emphasis during evaluative process is on the relationship of current work to previous work. The focus is on growth and on the next step of development. This type of evaluation is crucial during early creative experiences, and, to a degree, it is important at all levels of development. We must remember that the individual has tremendous capacity to be-

---

[8] Rogers, "Toward a Theory of Creativity," in *Creativity and Its Cultivation*, ed. Anderson, p. 80.

come increasingly competent in evaluating his own work and in setting goals for himself. The teacher must have faith in his ability to direct his own growth. More will be said about this aspect of evaluation in a later chapter.

Psychological freedom is as essential to the creator as psychological safety. Creativity thrives on freedom. Restrictions and pressures for conformity are stifling. Creative effort is nurtured best in an atmosphere that is permissive. As Rogers points out,

> This permissiveness gives the individual complete freedom to think, to feel, to be, whatever is most inward in himself. It fosters the openness, and the playful and spontaneous juggling of percepts, concepts, and meanings, which is a part of creativity.[9]

Permissiveness does not imply a complete lack of structure. Some framework is essential to protect the freedom as well as the psychological safety of the individual. Within this framework the learner should be free to select and develop his own ideas. He should sense that boundaries are flexible, not rigid. He should feel free to be himself and to create in his own way. As Harold Anderson says,

> Not every choice that the child makes is a critical experience, nor is every product of the child's originality a gem. What is important is the process of choosing and the process of producing. Through action comes a confidence by which a child knows that he is free to choose and free to produce his own contribution without threat, censor, or guilt from the environment.[10]

In summary, psychological safety and psychological freedom imply an atmosphere that is free, understanding, and stimulating. The working climate is permissive and reflects an interest in the individual. The activity is carried on as a cooperative effort and is a sharing process. Creative work is evaluated in terms of individual growth and not in comparison with others. Such an environment promotes a feeling of security and confidence that makes creative development possible.

DANCE EXPERIENCES THAT FOSTER CREATIVITY

The dancer who is interested in developing creatively must have many varied opportunities to use his imagination and to invent through the medium of movement. But rather than starting out by making full-blown dances, he should have many chances at first to create in small-structured problems. Creativity can be developed through

---

[9] Rogers, "Toward a Theory of Creativity," in *Creativity and Its Cultivation*, ed. Anderson, p. 80.

[10] *Creativity and Its Cultivation*, ed. Anderson, p. 133.

the exploration of movement material as well as through the organization of movement that leads to formed dances. The essential in each experience, exploring or forming, is an opportunity to be self-directed.

The very nature of the creative act makes choreographing a self-directed rather than an other-directed activity. No amount of meandering and meaningless self-direction will add up to a significant piece of choreography. But, on the other hand, no choreography will take shape without the special ingredient of self-direction. Dance should be experienced as an expressive activity and not as an imitative endeavor, because if one is to create dances he must be able to state himself. The dancer should grow steadily in understanding and skill so that his self-directed activity will not be aimless and will become more meaningful and mature.

If one accepts the creative approach to dance, then it follows that the study of movement as dance material must parallel, not precede, the creative experience. The technical and creative work should go hand in hand. Since the purpose of technique is to serve the needs of the creator, the technical study should grow out of the expressive needs. Technique should be studied and understood in relation to its ultimate purpose.

It is sometimes said that the beginning student is not ready to create. Although he may not be ready to create mature dances or even whole dances, creativity can take place at many levels, and the beginner is ready to respond imaginatively, even in the early experiences. It is through repeated opportunities for self-directed creative activity that the dancer develops his creative potential. The first creative experiences in dance may be broached with some degree of anxiety. The inexperienced dancer tends to feel hesitant and fearful of being different and incorrect. The strong need to conform is often the greatest obstacle confronting the individual who is trying to be creative. This hesitation should be understood, and experiences should be guided so that the student overcomes his fears.

Dance experiences that afford opportunity for self-directed activity and contribute to creative development can be classified under three major headings: exploration, improvisation, and composition. In each classification the activity should be structured so that it is appropriate to the individual's stage of development. Each creative effort should be challenging, but at the same time the task should be sensed as possible and comparatively safe to try. Those who wish to facilitate creative development in dance should understand each type of creative activity and know how to relate each to the various levels of creative development.

Exploring

Exploration involves thinking, imagining, feeling, and responding. In contrast to the imitative process, the self must direct the action response. Exploring is different from improvising and forming, inasmuch as the cues for action are externally motivated. In improvising and forming, the cues for action are internally motivated. For this reason, the exploring process can be extremely useful in the early dance experiences while the student still needs to be led out cautiously. Through the process of exploring, the usual pattern of following the teacher can be modified gradually so that the student becomes involved in the activity and is stimulated to make his own response. The following examples illustrate how the process can be applied to various dance experiences.

TORSO ACTION

The purpose of this exploration is to discover the flexion and extension action of the spine, with emphasis on sequential movement and full extension of the spine. The student sits on the floor with legs crossed tailor fashion, body relaxed forward, and arms hanging loosely at the side. He is asked to come to an upright position by starting the movement in the lower back and allowing it to progress up the back and through the head. (This is done without any demonstration.) Then he lets the body relax forward, and he repeats the upward movement.

After a few tries, the teacher, with the aid of a skeleton of the torso area, demonstrates the flexion and extension action of the spine and points out the relationship of the vertebrae to each phase of the action. Following the observation, the student is asked to relax forward and try the movement again. This time, with the eyes closed, the concentration is on the uncurling of the spine. The goal is to start in the lower back and bring up each vertebra one by one, trying not to skip a single one.

An observer might say, "Why go through all that? Couldn't you demonstrate the back extension and then let the student do it?" Yes, you could, but the result is different. The student can imitate the bent and upright position with little effort or concentration. He can arrive at the same general position, but the movement is not the same. In the method just described, the learner is deeply absorbed and highly conscious of the action. He gets "inside" the movement, so to speak. He understands the internal relationship and develops a kinesthetic awareness of the action. He is directing his own action as a means of solving a problem.

Because of the structure of the problem and the verbal cues supplied, the student has found the movement and has felt it. With additional cues he could go on to discover the feeling of qualities associated with this type of movement when it is motivated by the use of imagery, such as the texture of chiffon or the feeling of defiance. During the process of exploring he has felt "safe," or at least comparatively so. Working with the eyes closed helps him to concentrate and feel involved. He has found satisfaction in understanding the movement experience. These accomplishments are significant stepping stones in the process of developing creatively.

MOVEMENT QUALITIES

The purpose of this experience is to discover that movement quality depends on the use of energy and that the quality may be altered by changing either the amount of energy used or the nature of its release. The student is sitting on the floor, knees bent and legs turned out to one side. He is asked to imagine the following situation:

> You are sitting on the beach talking to a friend. It is a beautiful, warm, sunny day. As you sit there chatting and enjoying the sun, you toy with the sand by moving your foot back and forth and around. Close your eyes and imagine yourself in that situation. Go ahead.

This imagery will result in different responses, but in general the movement will tend to be slow and languid in nature. A different situation is then suggested to the student:

> You are still sitting and chatting, but this time as you move your feet about in the sand, a fly keeps annoying you by lighting on your leg or foot. Shut your eyes and try it.

This imagery will usually cause slow, languid movement to be interrupted by sharp, explosive action. Following the exploration, the teacher and students will then examine what has happened. They should look at the difference in the action response that resulted in one type of motivation, which caused the energy to be released slowly and continuously. The modified motivation was the fly, which caused the energy to be released suddenly and in varying amounts according to the degree of irritation. At this point, the teacher may wish to identify these movement qualities as "sustained" and "percussive."

This type of imagery experience can be extended by supplying different cues that cause the action to be transferred from the foot to the arm, the head, or the torso. Or the student may start with one part of the body and then shift the action as he wishes. This example of exploring points out again the way the student may be given an opportunity to create his own response and, at the same time, begin to discover the true meaning of movement quality and its expressive value.

BALANCE

The purpose of this experience is to heighten kinesthetic awareness of body alignment and the control of alignment during the process of shifting the center line of gravity. While the student is standing with the weight distributed equally over both feet, the teacher asks:

Where is the center line of gravity when you are standing in this position?

The class identifies it as a line running through the center of the body down between the feet and into the ground. The teacher assists with the clarification of this concept and then says:

Now without changing body alignment gradually shift the line of gravity so that it falls through the left foot. Be sure to maintain the feeling of the center and keep it controlled as you shift positions.

The teacher allows adequate time for the adjustment of weight and speaks in a manner that encourages the student to concentrate and attend to the action with a high degree of awareness:

Now slowly shift the line of gravity so that it falls through the right foot.

After a few repetitions vary the action by suggesting a step sidewards and then forward and backward. This sideward and forward action requires shifting farther from the original center. After students achieve some degree of accuracy and quality, the movement should be expanded. The teacher says:

Suppose that you move slowly but continuously to the left. Let your feet cross over, but be aware of centering with each step. Try it to the other side.

At a certain point a common rhythmic structure may be established and music introduced. The tempo can be varied but should be controlled, so that the speed does not destroy the concentration and accuracy. The students may try a structured pattern, such as three to the left and three to the right, or three to the left and five to the right. This pattern gives them a chance to see if they can maintain accuracy of alignment while shifting.

The success of experiences such as the ones described depends in large measure upon the teacher's understanding of the problem and ability to get students thoroughly involved in the activity. Without the right leadership, the experiences just described could be a waste of time. With skilled leadership the experiences can further the student's ability to direct his own action, to perceive the result of that action, and at the same time to learn fundamental movement principles.

Improvising

Improvisation offers greater opportunity for imagining, selecting, and creating than does exploration. Because there is more freedom there can be an increased amount of self-involvement. In this process the motivation supplies a stimulation that causes the self to respond and set up an inner action that finally results in the individual's unique response. The problem or situation that sets this process in action should be so structured that the boundaries are flexible and the individual is free to respond. Improvisation, if used wisely, can be a valuable means of furthering creative development. The movement activity that flows from improvisation is characterized by a spontaneity that is almost childlike in its naturalness. The imaginative power is at work. Actions go easily, and each new action sets off another one, which extends and expands the experience.

Creativity through improvisation has sometimes been referred to as the "flight into the unknown." It is the time when the creater draws upon stored images and brings forth new ones. Throughout this experience the creator is selecting, differentiating, contrasting, in the process of achieving integration and unity. From the improvisation experience comes a new awareness of the expressive nature of movement and of the integrity and rightness of the movement when you "let it happen" rather than arrange it. Perhaps the most amazing result for the individual is the realization that he invented and moved in a way that he thought was beyond his capacity. Again and again this type of experience seems to have the power to carry the individual beyond his usual level of performance.

A good improvisation experience is accompanied by satisfaction and a sense of fulfillment that is difficult to put into words. At the end of the experience, or during a fleeting moment within the experience, the creator feels a great sense of joy, a kind of ecstasy. Suddenly everything seems integrated, and he senses a unity that is profoundly satisfying. Fleeting or lasting, such an experience is fulfilling and contributes to the important prospect of self-actualization as well as the development in creativity.

Improvisation experiences in dance can be set in action in a variety of ways. For example, one might use as the means of motivation basic movement patterns that have been learned, or sensory perception, or a specific situation. Whatever approach is used, the problem should be planned so that it is appropriate for the individual's level of psychological readiness. The following illustrations suggest various ways that improvisation may be included in the dance experience.

BASIC MOVEMENT PATTERN

Improvisation can grow out of certain movements that have been learned. The student's primary concern in such improvisation is with manipulating material rather than inventing material. He makes choices and uses material in his own way. This type of creative experience is especially good for novices. The two examples that follow illustrate how creativity can develop in relation to technical study.

Sliding through space. This improvisation experience should follow the initial learning of the basic movement pattern of sliding. The technical emphasis is on the use of the feet, elevation, and rebound. The purpose of the improvisation is to increase motivation and to provide experience in self-directed activity. Creativity may be encouraged as follows:

> *This time as you move across the floor start with the left side leading. Change from left to right when you feel like it. Try to shift several times. What other directions could you use?*
>
> Reply—*Diagonally, sidewards.*
>
> *Try this time to use different directions. Try at least two and shift the leading side whenever you want to. Is there any additional direction that could be introduced as you progress across the floor?*
>
> Reply—*Around in a circle.*
>
> *Let's add a circular path to the possibilities. Start in any direction. Change whenever you like, but try to use a circular path at least once.*

This illustration shows how improvisation can be related to movement pattern. Asking students for suggestions or possibilities stimulates them to think for themselves. Although dialogue does not indicate repetition and the reworking of ideas in relation to movement needs, this should occur. In this experience the technical aspect of movement is combined with creative effort. Improvisation that requires a student to make decisions about direction and the side that leads is a good first step in self-directed activity. Experiences such as this can speed up learning and increase students' satisfaction. Sometimes the beginning student is quite amazed at his ability to manipulate and be inventive with basic movement material.

Descending to the floor and recovering. Improvisation in this area would follow movement studies that focus on experiencing the "giving in" to the pull of gravity and descending (falling) to the floor. The purpose of this improvisation is to relate the principles of descending and recovering to a movement problem and therefore make the technical aspects of the movement become more functional. The essence of falling movement must become a part of the individual so that he uses it in his own way for expressive purposes. A shift in focus from the technical phase to self-directed activity and improvisation might be achieved in the following manner:

> *Imagine that there is a force that pulls you into the floor. Your resistance to the pull causes you to shift your standing position. You may wish to move sideward or around, but finally you are pulled into the floor. Go ahead and try it. Take as much time as you need.*
>
> *Now visualize the movement of some object such as the tail of a kite, a tumbleweed, or a chiffon scarf as it floats in the air. Select one of these objects. Imagine that it is wafted into the air, then comes to rest momentarily on the ground, and again is lifted into the air. Now as you let your movement carry you into the floor and up again, concentrate on the action of the object and try to capture the essence of its quality or feeling in your movement.*
>
> *This time let the descending and recovering happen as you progress across the floor. Move as fast or as slowly as you like. At some point include a sustained turn of some kind and let that movement carry you into the floor and out again. Start with a walk and then proceed in your own way. Go ahead.*

Imagery problems such as these affect the use of tension and thus the quality and timing of the movement sequence. The results may be interesting enough to go on with other suggestions that change the dynamics and build the movement dramatically. The ultimate purpose is to make techniques of descending functional in an expressive way. Through this process, the student has a chance to work creatively.

SENSORY PERCEPTION

Another type of improvisation can be stimulated through sensory response. In this case no specific movement patterns are used as a starting point. The improvisation stems from the sensory response that is transposed rather spontaneously into movement. In this type of movement, it is important that the proper mood be set so that the individual becomes absorbed in the experience and can respond sensitively and kinesthetically. In some instances, the individual will move more easily if his eyes are closed, since elimination of the visual stimuli makes concentration easier. The following examples illustrate the use of sound and objects as a means of stimulating sensory response.

Sounds. Students are sitting on the floor close together but with adequate room to move. Percussion instruments of varied tone quality and pitch, such as a drum, wood block, gong, maraca, sandpaper block, and ratchet are nearby. The teacher explains that the experience is concerned with experimenting with different sounds, discovering how they feel, and moving in relation to the feeling response. She says:

> *Most of our day is spent in thinking and making decisions. For the next few minutes let's eliminate the thinking. Don't try to be intellectual. Let's concern ourselves with feelings. You will concentrate on the sounds and your feeling response to them. Let your movement come spontaneously. Use any part of the body, arms, legs, torso, head, but don't try to think or plan. Let the movement happen as you feel. Close your eyes and try it.*

Usually it is a good idea to experiment with two or three sounds. Then have the student open his eyes. Make some brief comment that will help him concentrate on the feeling. Then continue with the eyes closed. Sounds of each instrument can be used several times before shifting to contrasting sounds. Though it is usually better to break the activity with a comment or two and then continue with the experience, there should always be enough time in each experience for students to become absorbed. Of course, the teacher must sustain the mood and concentration throughout the total experience.

As soon as the student begins to concentrate and move freely, the teacher may wish to extend the experience by suggesting:

> *Explore the space that is around you;*

or

> *Try letting the movement carry you up to your knee or to your feet.*

This type of experience can be used as preparation for a short, creative study. For example, two contrasting sounds can be selected and used as motivation. It is better to work from the memory of sounds and feeling, since this approach helps to keep the experience at a kinesthetic level.

Inanimate objects. A great variety of objects can be useful in stimulating a sensory response and movement improvisation. For example, suppose a piece of driftwood or a feather is used as motivation. The teacher may use questions such as the following as a means of helping students to see the object and feel its texture:

What do you see? Is it smooth? Are there differences in the tension quality?

After a short period of observation, the student is ready to improvise. Then after a brief period of experimentation, it may be wise to sustain the improvisation long enough for the student to find a phrase or motif that he likes. This motif can then be used as a starting point from which other movements evolve. This material can be used as the basis for an organized study or dance.

SITUATIONS

Improvisation may be approached through the use of a specific situation. This type of creative problem prompts a recall of life experiences. Stored images act as a springboard for new, imaginative responses. The self, interacting with these responses, creates a solution that is dynamic and unique.

Chance meeting. A situation such as chance meeting can stimulate improvisation. For example, suppose two students are moving at the same time from opposite corners of the room. As they use the locomotor movement that they know, they pass each other at some midpoint. This action is repeated several times until they are accustomed to the movement pattern.

A variation of this exercise can be to start with the same locomotor pattern but change the action by introducing a situation that provides a new motivation. For instance, the emphasis may now be on the "meeting and passing" of the other person. The encounter should be an important event. The meeting may be characterized by excitement or haste. Each pair should be encouraged to take time to react to the other person and to make something of the encounter before going on across the floor.

This type of problem encourages spontaneity. Even though the improvisation has a brief existence, there is time to experiment with fresh movement and to become aware of moving in relation to another moving body. As dancers become comfortable with improvisation and are able to sustain concentration, they will enjoy improvising around some dramatic situation that involves three or four persons. The problem of relating to more than one person adds another dimension to the experience.

"Against" and "with" a situation. The purpose of the improvisation is to sustain imagery and develop movement ideas. To sustain and develop improvisation, the individual must be prepared for the experience. He needs to explore the problem in various ways and become totally involved with the idea. As an example, the student may first

transpose feelings into drawings, then into movement, and finally into an abstracted situation. The students are seated on the floor near the piano. Each person has several large sheets of newsprint and two different-colored pieces of chalk.

The teacher says:

Suppose we concentrate on feeling relationships—the feelings that result from interactive forces. Most of the time we are experiencing some kind of feeling response to objects, to people, and to happenings, or to ourselves. These are everyday occurrences. Now imagine some of these forces at play, and try to capture the essence of the feeling in movement. Sometimes we feel very much opposed to an object or person. We feel against them. Other times we feel very warmly toward them, or feel with them. Imagine a situation where the feeling is strongly against or opposed. Let the chalk carry your feelings onto the paper. Close your eyes. Concentrate on your image. Go ahead.

This time imagine a situation where you feel warmly toward the object, or very much with the person. Concentrate on your image. Go ahead.

It may be worthwhile to repeat some of the experiences. Usually it requires more than one trial to "get into the feeling." Working with the eyes closed helps the individual make a sensitive response and avoid planned patterns. It may be useful to make a third drawing in which the individual shifts from one image to the other, sometimes motivated by the feeling of *with,* and sometimes *against.*

As a next step, have students work without the chalk and try moving with the whole body. Have them experiment with the same feelings of with and against. Have students try each motivation separately and then shift from one to the other. Expand the movement so that the legs, arms, and all parts of the body are involved. Experiment with music as a background and then work without music.

Now change the settings so that the students are standing around the room and are free to move. Place two or three drums at various spots in the center floor area. The drums may be used as imagined objects or situations. The problem is still related to transposing the feeling of with or against into movement, but this time with emphasis on development of the movement ideas. The teacher says:

Start moving around the room and establish a relationship with one of the objects. Set up some imagery as you relate to the object. You may move away from it temporarily and then return to it. You may want to move in and strike the object. Move in the way that feels right to you. When you have some movement idea established, try to develop it and carry it through to a resolution. Start with the walk. Go ahead.

In summary, improvisation is one kind of creative endeavor. It can be used in connection with the learning of movement patterns or as a preparatory step in composition. The process of improvising is of particular value because it stimulates the imagination, which, of course, is an essential ingredient in the creative act. Because this type of experience encourages fresh movement response, it fosters the development of creativity.

The indiscriminate use of improvisation, however, can be defeating. Only if it is used wisely will it contribute to creativity. Just as it has potential to stimulate imaginative action, it also can be a powerful force that inhibits the individual and blocks his learning. As was stated earlier, the human being is hesitant and cautious about revealing his inner self. If he is placed in situations that ask for too much too soon, he may withdraw rather than give out.

Experiences that depend on imaginative responses and deep self-involvement must start at a very simple level and and progress gradually as the student gains confidence and skill. Students should start with structured problems and move slowly toward the open and less structured ones. In other words, the improvisation experience should become more demanding and have greater freedom for individual responses as the individual is ready to "risk himself" and to find satisfaction in so doing. The student's readiness determines the appropriateness of the experience. There is only one way for the teacher to identify such readiness and that is through his empathy with the student's creative activity.

The two types of self-directed dance experiences identified as exploring and improvising are stepping stones that lead toward the discovery of a full creative act. The intent of this section has been to suggest that even though the student may not be ready to create a mature dance, he is ready to think, feel, and respond on his own at a primary level, and such experiences are essential for creative development. In other words, creative development results from activity that encourages creative responses.

Forming

The ultimate goal in the self-directed experience is to create a dance. This process is called composing, or *forming*. The need to compose springs from the human being's desire to give form to that which he discovers. Spontaneity is still important, but to spontaneity is added the process of selecting, integrating, and unifying. The result of this process is more than random movement. The product has form. The new entity is called a dance. The organized movement becomes a symbolic form, a dance that presents the unique expression of the creator.

The demands of composing are greater than those of the spontaneous improvisation. The composed work requires control as well as imaginative thrust. In the creation of the great dance composition, time, patience, and a great deal of hard work are required. The inspiration may come like a flash, but to mold the final product in such a way that it captures the essence of the creator's image may take considerable effort. The level of creativity and ability needed to choreograph mature works is attained only after many lesser dances have been composed. This aspect of dance composition will be discussed more fully in chapter five.

DEVELOPING CREATIVITY TAKES TIME

Developing creativity is a highly personal matter and cannot be rushed. Each individual must have opportunities that allow him to develop the understandings, skill, and confidence needed for this aspect of behavior called "creativity." Because creative growth is so dependent on the self-response of the creator, it is unpredictable. It does not follow any set order or time pattern. Sometimes progress is slow, and other times the individual advances in spurts. Development may reach a plateau or even seem to regress. No two persons will develop at the same rate or in the same way. But this should not seem strange. How could it be otherwise, when creativity depends on the unique perception and expression of the self?

Each individual must be allowed to progress through the various stages of development. Teachers are tempted sometimes to try to pass on some of their own understanding and thus hasten the student's progress. It doesn't work that way. Real understanding and skill must be acquired through experience; the student must learn through his discovery. Each new, differentiated aspect of learning must be integrated with and seen in relation to the individual's total concept of dance. Only in this way does he increase his perception, which is the foundation for creativity. His first studies may be naïve and a bit personal, but the true sophisticated work can come only through experience. Some individuals can progress at a faster rate than others, and the teacher's task is to help each develop as rapidly as he can.

Those who wish to facilitate creativity should try to surround and immerse the learner with stimulation that causes creative action. This is the challenge for the teacher. What could be more important than facilitating the creative development of the human being?

SUMMARY

The human being has the unique capacity to think and act creatively, an ability that makes possible his reaching out for the unknown. It is believed that all individuals have potential capacity to create, although some persons seem to have more innate ability than others. There is some evidence that highly creative individuals possess certain characteristics such as openness to new experiences, capacity to be puzzled, aesthetic sensitivity, imagination, and extensive creative energy. However, each individual should be encouraged to develop his creative ability to its fullest extent. In order to develop, he must have many opportunities to create and thus expand his insight, skill, and confidence.

Dance as an art experience is concerned with creativity. Even the beginner should be encouraged to make imaginative responses and to self-direct activity. The creative response can be attained through the process of exploration and improvisation, as well as through composition problems that provide an opportunity for the dancer to think, feel, imagine, and create. The creative aspect of dance should start early and be experienced continually. The individual's creative growth depends on experience and time to develop. He must have opportunity to progress from the simple to the complex. The demands of each creative problem should be related to the creator's level of development.

Creativity flourishes best in an environment that is permissive. The creator needs to feel that he is free to respond in his own way. The psychological factors of safety and freedom, along with a sympathetic understanding of the facilitating person, seem to significantly affect the individual's progress and creativity.

A student dancer shows how costume and light can highlight movement.
Photograph by Pete Salutos.

three

Increasing aesthetic awareness

Any art object, including a dance, becomes an organic entity as the result of the sensitive integration of all its components. As Suzanne Langer says,

> An artistic symbol is a much more intricate thing than we usually think of as form, because it involves all the relationships of its elements to one another, all similarities and differences of quality, not only the geometric and other familiar relations.[1]

In dance the aesthetic elements may be identified as "virtual forces," or more specifically, as space tensions, rhythmic tensions, and movement tensions. These aesthetic elements of space, time, and force do not exist in isolation or as separate entities but rather as interacting forces. It is through the interplay and relationship of these forces that dance is unified and achieves its expressive and communicative value.

AESTHETIC GROWTH IN DANCE

Aesthetic growth implies increased ability to bring about harmonious organization of the elements of the dance. This growth is fos-

---

[1] Suzanne K. Langer, *Feeling and Form* (New York: Charles Scribner's Sons, 1953), p. 51.

tered through an education of the senses that enables the individual to reach into his world for the unfamiliar and to respond with aesthetic sensitivity. He learns first to make aesthetic discovery and second to assimilate that which is discovered.

Aesthetic growth, like creative development, must have time to unfold and mature. The dancer must have many opportunities to explore his dance material in terms of his personal responses to his world and the aesthetic element of his art medium. Since aesthetic growth does not follow any specific pattern and may start in unpredictable ways, the nature of the learning experience is of greater importance than the sequence. The dancer needs experiences in three major areas of development, which include (1) awareness of sensory data and ability to experience fully; (2) ability to use aesthetic elements of dance in relation to a specific motivation; and (3) competence in making aesthetic judgments in the process of composing so that the result is aesthetically satisfying.

Aesthetic growth can take place out of class as well as in class. Students should be encouraged to take advantage of all experiences. For example, art exhibits, concerts, the theater, good literature, and nature are all sources of experiences that increase aesthetic awareness.

Within the class much can be done to increase sensitivity and appreciation by calling attention to aesthetic stimuli, such as a piece of sculpture that shows tension qualities, a painting that makes certain use of space relationship, and music that depicts rhythmic contrast.

Aesthetic experiences are usually perceived as Gestalts. The separate elements impinge upon each other, and we react to the total event or experience. We may, and frequently do, go beyond this first perception and make a special effort to "lift out" certain aspects of the sensory experience for exploration and gratification. In dance, too, the total perception is often followed by the lifting out of a single element. The aesthetic elements of force, space, and time are interlocking; dance never exists without the presence of all three. And yet for purposes of aesthetic education it is desirable and even necessary to concentrate on one element at a time. This kind of focused attention helps the dance student to differentiate and see each element in its relationship to the whole of dance. Let us turn, then, to a discussion of each aesthetic element and its functional relationship to choreography.

FORCE AS AN AESTHETIC ELEMENT

The aesthetic quality of dance movement is determined by the flow and control of energy. Energy, or force, is the source of movement, and it is also the basic ingredient in the aesthetic qualities of dance. The choreographer controls the dynamic flow of the dance through a sensitive organization of movement tension. The play of forces set in action by the structured movement tension evokes a kinesthetic response in the perceiver and thus enables the dancer to communicate. The tension aspects of the movement cause the observer to empathize or "feel into" the dance and thus perceive its import.

As John Martin has said,

> It is the dancer's whole function to lead us into imitating his action with our faculty of inner mimicry in order that we may experience his feeling. Facts he could tell us, but feelings he could not convey in any other way than by arousing them in us through sympathetic response.[2]

Movement qualities

The quality of movement can be controlled in two ways: (1) by varying the amount of energy expended; and (2) by releasing energy in different ways. When a great amount of energy is used, we think of movement as being strong, possessing a high degree of tension. When a minimum amount of energy is expended, we think of the movement as weak and lacking in tension.

By controlling the amount of energy and its release, the dancer can achieve quite different qualities. These qualities are identified as sustained, percussive, vibratory, or swinging movement. For example, when energy is released evenly and continuously, movement is *sustained.* Sustained movement gives the feeling of smoothness and "continuity," as exemplified by a push-pull action.

When energy is expended suddenly, however, the movement will appear sharp and jerky. This *percussive* type of action may be the sudden thrust of the arm, the quick twist of the torso, or the explosive jump in the air. The explosive or percussive action may be modified by releasing the energy in small spurts with great rapidity and regularity. The result is a *vibratory* or shaking action. This kind of movement stimulates a feeling of excitement and sometimes of suspense.

When the impulse and momentum that cause this action are allowed to continue to the point of energy depletion before the new impetus sets off the return movement, *swinging* action results. At the height of this pendular action, there is a moment of suspension (balance in mid-air) before the release and the new impetus takes over. Swinging movement tends to have a soothing and relaxing effect. However, the movement can

---

2 John Martin, *Introduction to Dance* (New York: W. W. Norton & Company, Inc., 1939), p. 53.

be breath-taking and emotionally exciting when the point of suspension is fully realized.

Approaches to the study of movement quality

Force as an aesthetic element can be studied in various ways. The following illustrations suggest approaches that may be used to increase aesthetic awareness and, also, to develop skill in creating movement qualities appropriate to the aesthetic intent. These are presented as samples and are not intended as a formula.

AWARENESS OF MOVEMENT TENSION

To increase kinesthetic awareness of tension and its aesthetic value, one needs to "feel" tension in his own body. A verbal description is not an adequate means of acquiring full awareness of quality. An individual cannot judge accurately the amount of tension in his movement until he has discovered the feeling of tension in varying amounts. An individual may think that his movement has a great deal of tension, whereas another person may judge it to be only moderately tense.

Moving with, and in relation to, objects of varying weights helps the dance student to experience the feel of tension. He might try to push some very heavy object such as a piano and then, in contrast, some very light object. Two individuals may resist one another by facing and placing the palms of the right hands against each other with arms extended. Both persons should resist and try to outpush each other. Through this experience they will feel tension in the arm and shoulder and, to some degree, in the whole body. Another possibility is to use a partner as a dead weight to be lifted or pulled. In experiences such as these the student should be encouraged to attend to the kinesthetic feel. As he gains increased awareness, he will be able to recall the sensation and establish the same tension states or modified states according to his purpose.

Imagery is another excellent means of experiencing tension states. For example, have students try moving with the images in mind of walking in deep sand or of floating like a feather in the air. Images such as these may be the motivation for short improvisations that will call for various tension states and, thus, different movement qualities. Sometimes there is value in observing the movement responses of others. Visual perception increases awareness of the differences in the kinesthetic response to movement qualities motivated by various images. The visual and kinesthetic demonstration helps to increase understanding of the value of force as an aesthetic element in expression.

Imagery may be used as the motivation for dance study that goes beyond the improvisational stage. Consider the movement possibilities stimulated by the image of a wide and very strong rubber band. Have the students imagine that the powerful band is around their wrists holding them closely together. Have them try to stretch the bands so that they can move the wrists and the arms apart in different directions. They should work slowly at first, moving the wrists as far as possible, then moving as quickly as the imagined band will allow. They should sometimes release the tension quickly so that the wrists return suddenly. Other times the release should be controlled so that the return is gradual. Combine the various possibilities, and then let the movement extend to the torso and neck, as well as to other parts of the body.

The teacher can guide the preceding explorations by inserting cues during the action or by setting the problem carefully and provocatively before the action begins. The student should be encouraged to attend to the kinesthetic sensation associated with the movement, since the purpose of the experience is to increase the feel or awareness of tension. Experiences such as these should be followed by discussion of the relationship of movement qualities and kinesthetic response to the process of creating dances.

EXPERIENCING MOVEMENT QUALITY

Although achieving kinesthetic awareness of feeling states is essential, the dancer must also understand how to control quality in order to achieve bold or subtle aesthetic results. The imitation method has been used as one means of discovering and controlling movement qualities. In this method the student observes a specific quality and then tries to move in the same manner. The visual stimulation that results from a good demonstration can be a successful means of motivating the learning experience, but it is probably not always the best method.

Demonstration is usually more effective when it is used as an important adjunct to instruction rather than as the primary means of teaching. Somehow we have to find a more powerful way to "get inside" the learner than the visual method provides. Repetition in an unthinking and unfeeling manner does not result in a meaningful experience. There must be internal experiencing by the muscles, the nervous system, and the total person. This is not to say that demonstrations are worthless. On the contrary, they have their place along with many other visual devices. But the demonstration that relies on visual sensation is only one means of stimulating learning. Often the demonstration is most useful when it follows an exploratory action motivated by stimuli that are not visual. This is especially true in the study of the force of movement, because movement quality must be motivated internally in order to attain its fullest expressive power.

How then can internally motivated movement experiences be stimulated in the dance situation? The examples included in the following section illustrate two approaches: (1) the use of problem situations solved through self-directed responses; and (2) the use of imagery and motivation that evoke a feeling response. These examples do not prescribe the full teaching process but simply suggest ways of motivating sustained, percussive, swinging, and vibratory movement.

Basic movement. The first two examples suggest ways to relate quality to basic movement study. In this first instance, torso extension is used. Students are sitting either with legs to the side or crosslegged. They follow the verbal cues of the teacher. Each person initiates his own response. No demonstration is used.

The teacher says:

> *Slowly extend the spine upward until you reach the highest point; then slowly return to the starting position. Start the movement at the base of the spine and progress upward continuously. Breathe in with the extension and out with the release of tension. . . . Move in the same way, but this time have the action take place very quickly as though you were startled. Return quickly. Now try making the upward movement very explosive. Let it happen all at once; then return slowly and continuously. Reverse the action. Make the upward movement continuous and easy, and then return with a sudden pull that gets you down all at once.*

At this point the teacher might initiate discussion about these two types of movement—sustained and percussive—and the feel of each. Half the class might observe the other half in action, in order to discover their kinesthetic response to different qualities. Following the observation some generalization should be made about the energy relationships to movement quality.

Another example of the basic movement approach is the use of swinging movement. The teacher says:

> *In standing position with feet slightly apart, body lifted upward, and arms stretched overhead, as you breathe out, release the tension slowly so that the knees become soft and the torso and arms drop forward easily. The neck should be relaxed and the head should be dangling. Now breathe in slowly as you extend the torso and the arms upward. Do this gradually but fully. Repeat the action. Try to get the feeling of full extension and then the release. This time move in the same way, but give a feeling of impetus and flow. At the bottom of the descent, just when the movement comes to the*

point of stillness, give a new impetus that causes the upward action. Allow the movement to reach its fullest height and suspend there for a moment before the downward action takes over.

Following the exploration, make comments that help convey the idea of impetus, suspension, and release of the swinging action. The tendency of the beginner is to stop the action, rather than let it expend itself, so that he fails to experience the relationship between the movement momentum and the gravity pull. A good demonstration might be helpful at this point to emphasize the relaxation at the lowest point and the suspension at the height of action.

Now the teacher may say:

Now try the swinging action in a sideward movement. Start with the torso and the arms extended sideward horizontally. Release the tension and allow the relaxed body to fall to center position. Then with a new impetus, direct the movement to the other side. Allow time to capture the moment of suspension at the top of the swing and then continue.

During the attempts at sideward swinging movement, certain technical problems, such as the sequential action of the spine, the body facing, and the action, may need attention. After the basic action is established, continue the movement exploration in different directions, such as forward and diagonally forward. Also, try varying the height and range of the swing, as well as the speed. Experiencing the swinging quality in different ways and in different parts of the body contributes to a functional understanding of quality as an aesthetic element.

Sometimes students, through previous experiences, have come to know swinging movement not as a quality but as a movement pattern that "swings from side to side and then around overhead." This kind of technical performance is superficial and does not provide an adequate foundation for creative work.

Objects as props. People enjoy experimenting with objects which often can be used as a good source of motivation. In the following examples a rope is used to feel tension and to discover movement qualities. Each pair of students is provided with a short cotton rope about seven feet long.

Students *A* and *B* sit on the floor facing each other. Each holds one end of the rope. They should be far enough apart that the rope is kept taut. Student *A* is instructed to pull continuously during counts 1 and 2, while student *B* resists the pull. The movement is reversed on counts 3 and 4, with *B* pulling and *A* resisting. Repeat the action several times at a fairly slow tempo. Then vary the movement by making the pull longer, increasing the count, or exploring different directions. This even flow of energy results in sustained quality.

Then use a quick two-count movement. Complete the pull on count 1 and hold on count 2. Students A and B continue taking turns at pulling. The person who is resisting will need to be alert to avoid being pulled off balance. This action results in percussive movement.

Now combine the sustained and percussive movements. The active person may move continuously or abruptly. Use music in the background, so that students have freedom to vary the duration of each movement. Encourage them to modify the spatial range of the movement. Students should continue taking turns as active and resistant participants.

Next introduce a third use of energy which results in a vibratory quality. Have students A and B sit facing each other, each holding the rope with one hand. They should sit far enough apart that the rope is fully extended (not taut) and is resting on the floor. Working simultaneously, A and B give the rope small successive pulls to the right and then to the left. They increase the speed at which they are shaking the rope so that it ripples on the floor. This movement performed rapidly causes the hand and arms to vibrate. Have students repeat the action with the other arm.

Now repeat the foregoing movement, but at some point have the students drop the rope and continue the vibrating action without it. Then have them pick up the rope again, perhaps with the other hand, and continue vibrating. Have students alternately drop the rope and pick it up, sustaining the shaking action at all times. A variation is to start the action in the same manner, first with the rope and then without it, but then to alter the movement by such verbal cues as: "Arm in back of you" or "The leg higher than your head."

This type of experience, which explores the use of energy in various ways, is stimulating and results in amazing quality responses. At this point the teacher may want to identify and discuss the different qualities and give the student an opportunity to use qualities in an improvisational way. For example, students might continue to work with the rope but would control the duration, direction, and tempo in their own way. Action might be shifted from one to the other by one's sensing the completion of his partner's movement. The inactive person should continue to provide some degree of resistance in order to keep the exercise a tension study. Without this emphasis, it might turn into a design study, which would be quite another problem.

The improvisation may be followed by a problem or dance study.

For example, the problem might be to use at least two movement quali-ties in an interesting spatial relationship. The problem should provide an opportunity to experiment with quality as an aesthetic element and to work toward a result that is unified and kinesthetically satisfying.

Sensory stimuli. In the preceding examples students have been con-sciously aware of energy release. The following illustrations reverse the process and get at movement quality in an indirect fashion through the use of different types of motivation. The student's sensory response to stimuli determines the quality of movement.

For instance, sounds of the human voice can be interesting and stim-ulating sources of movement. Have students use nonsense syllables or just utter sounds. Vary the volume and intensity, and let the movement happen with the sound. The breath relationship as well as energy and feeling relationships will influence the quality. The use of sound evokes full responses and movement that is organic in the true sense.

The visual stimuli provided by an object—its shape, line, and texture —may be used as motivation. Also, the action of certain objects such as an egg beater or carrousel stimulate imaginative movement responses. Then, of course, nature provides many sources of sensory stimulation. For example, the quality of delicate leaves, gnarled branches, or the spray of the ocean can be inspiration for movement.

Gestures. Gestures related to certain characterizations or situations often result in imaginative responses that reveal movement quality. For example, have students explore the gesture of shaking hands. First, have them shake hands as they would in everyday life. Then they take a step forward as though being introduced to someone and pantomime the handshake. Next they use the gesture as dance material. The fol-lowing situations might be used as sources of imagery: (1) a girl being introduced to a queen; (2) a teenage boy being introduced to a girl; and (3) an elderly person greeting an old friend. The movement pattern that results from each motivation has a distinct quality and feeling tone. The quality is inherent in the imagery and movement response.

Word symbols. Word symbols will also motivate movement that emphasizes quality. For example, choose a word such as "burdened." Have students think of the characteristic feelings of one who is burdened. The feelings, of course, depend on the cause of the burden and on the individual who is burdened. The response to "burden" might be anxiety or anticipation, weariness or hopefulness, nervousness or languidness. After examining various possibilities through discussion, have students explore some of them through improvisation. Then select one aspect or one kind of burden quality and use that as the specific motivation form to study. The purpose of a study like this one is to capture the essence of a feeling quality rather than to pantomime a specific person who is experiencing that feeling.

Summary

The examples presented in the preceding paragraphs illustrate varied approaches to the study of movement quality as an aesthetic element. These approaches range from the self-directed analytical process to the use of imagery and other types of motivation that evoke sensory responses. Some experiences primarily help the student get the kinesthetic feel of the energy element of movement, whereas other experiences provide qualitative material that may be extended and developed into dance studies.

Force as an aesthetic element must be experienced many times and in varying contexts. It is through experiencing that the choreographer heightens his sensitivity, increases kinesthetic awareness in movement qualities, and becomes more skillful in creating dance form that captures his feeling responses.

SPACE AS AN AESTHETIC ELEMENT

The spatial element of dance has an inherent relationship to the motor forces and rhythmic structure of the movement pattern. In fact, the movement caused by the motor forces molds the spatial aspects of dance and makes space come alive as an aesthetic element. Space design and dance structure evolve together as a direct result of motivation and the image of the choreographer.

The spectator is made aware of space and space-force relationships in dance only when there is action. Until there is something going on in space, the perceiver has little or no awareness of this element. Speaking about the relationships between space and space-force, Rudolph Arnheim states that

> . . . the space of a theatre or dance stage is defined by the motor forces that populate it. Expanse becomes real when the dancer runs across it; distance is created by actors withdrawing from each other; and the particular qualities of the central location are brought to light when embodied forces strive for it, rest at it, rule from it.[3]

---

[3] Rudolf Arnheim, *Art and Visual Perception* (Berkeley: University of California Press, 1960), p. 309.

Therefore, the aesthetic value of space is dependent on the dancer's ability to define and control it in such a way that it heightens the kinesthetic impact and, thus, the meaning of the dance as a whole.

Space-time-force relationships

The effectiveness of the space-movement relationship in furthering aesthetic purpose is influenced significantly by the rhythmic structure or time aspects of the movement that causes the change in space. The interdependence of movement, time, and space is fundamental to the nature of dance. As Lauterer has pointed out, these three aspects compose a meaningful triad of sensation, and it is almost impossible to isolate one of them and create an artistic expression.

> Space is motionless and silent until movement within it introduces time and thereby gives space a voice, a specific expression relative to the tempo and dynamic time of the movement.[4]

The duration of the movement or action in space influences the perception of space. Movement causes something to happen and thus brings about a change in the conditions of the environment. This change is sensed as having a duration and is perceived in terms of time. In other words, time may be thought of as the dimension of change. Only as time is consumed does change occur. It is change and the sequence of changes that are perceived by the observer. The total effect of the changes is experienced as a happening—a dance happening.

The choreographer must be able to use the energized movement of the body to cause changes in spatial and action design, and thus create space-force tensions that are perceived as dynamic forces. The perceiver's feeling response is evoked not by the design alone, but rather by the forces created by space-movement relationship. Arnheim refers to these visible motor forces in this way:

> When an object moves, we often see more than simple displacement. The object is perceived as being acted upon by forces; in fact, it is the presence of perceptual forces that gives expression to motion.[5]

The choreographer's success, then, depends on his ability to conceive space-force relationships and to control them imaginatively. The subsequent section is a discussion of how this kind of sensitivity and competence can be developed.

---

[4] Arch Lauterer, "The Discovery of Art in Oneself through Movement, Time, and Space," in *Impulse*, ed. Marian Van Tuyl (San Francisco: Impulse Publications, Inc., 1959), p. 51.

[5] Arnheim, *Art and Visual Perception*, p. 321.

Photograph by Silvily Kessler.

Attributes of space design

Before the creator can work imaginatively with space, he must know the inherent characteristics of movement design. For example, spatial balance, direction, and dimension are significant attributes of all spatial design and therefore are related to choreography. But above all, the choreographer must know that dance movement and therefore space design have to be motivated. In other words, the dance form, including the spatial aspects of the structure, must follow motivation, not precede it. The total design must evolve because of, and in relation to, motivation. When this evolution does not occur, the movement is empty and meaningless, and the dance is nothing more than a series of poses or unrelated movements devoid of aesthetic value. On the other hand, when movement ideas and organized form spring from motivation, the spatial design emerges as a dynamic element of the dance.

SPATIAL BALANCE

Balance is the prime factor in space perception. One aspect of spatial balance is determined by the relationship of the body to the pull of gravity through the vertical, diagonal, or horizontal planes. Each plane, because of its peculiar relationship to gravity, achieves a different state of balance and has a different dynamic value. Space-body-gravity relationships can be created so that they evoke the feeling of tension or relaxation, of activity or quiet, and of danger or security.

For example, movement in the vertical plane is sensed as stable. It is alive but contained. The observer does not worry about the balance of the dancer as long as the body maintains a vertical relationship to gravity. This is so even when fast movement, such as a spirited jump, propels the body directly upward.

Quite a different feeling response occurs, however, as one perceives the body shift from the vertical to the diagonal plane. Immediately one senses a deviation from the norm and a feeling of imbalance and insecurity. As the diagonal plane moves farther away from the vertical, tension is increased, and not until the movement begins to approximate or reach the horizontal plane does the perceiver feel a sense of stability. The greatest tension is experienced at the point of greatest imbalance between the vertical and horizontal. Movement that deviates from the stable plane (diagonal movement) is charged with energy and is sensed as dynamic. Movement in this plane appears to have a sense of urgency and striving for resolution.

Movement in the horizontal plane is also associated with a feeling of stability. However, the horizontal tends to convey a feeling of expansiveness in contrast to the collectedness of the vertical. Frequently movement in the horizontal may be perceived as calm and restful and not as alive as that of the vertical. But the primary feeling of the horizontal, as well as of the vertical plane, is that of stability and security.

An understanding of the aesthetic value of different states of balance achieved through the various use of planes is essential for creative work in dance. The dance student should be allowed to explore movement in all planes. He needs to observe movement patterns that make use of different planes. Through observation he senses the inherent tension and discovers the aesthetic value of various states of balance. Also, there is value in observing what happens to the force relationship when a movement pattern is altered in various ways. For example, have students take the movement pattern that emphasizes the vertical plane and modify the movement so that it is performed on a diagonal plane. Then alter the rhythmic pattern and speed and observe the difference in the kinesthetic impact of the various spatial and rhythmic organizations.

Another means of increasing understanding of the dynamic value of the different states of balance is through the exploration of various ways of falling or giving in to gravity. Sometimes students think of falls as specific patterns or techniques to be learned. Such an approach is unfortunate, because it is important for the student to discover the kinesthetic value of movement that shifts from the stability of the vertical, through the imbalance of the diagonal, to the security of the horizontal. The student should experience the suspense that is created as the body moves through the state of imbalance. He should be aware of the difference in the kinesthetic impact of descent when it moves through a forward, sideward, backward, and circular path.

Sometimes it is beneficial to concentrate on a specific pattern of falling in order to gain technical skill needed to control the body in space. The technical proficiency, however, should be a means to the end. The ultimate goal should be to increase awareness of dynamic states of imbalance and to develop skill in creating and controlling movement so that it achieves the tensional qualities needed to communicate.

Another kind of spatial balance is the impression of overall balance that is inherent in a specific movement or a total movement design (that is, symmetry or asymmetry). Each type of organization, symmetrical and asymmetrical, achieves its overall sense of spatial balance in a different way. Each creates a unique space-force relationship and hence has a different kinesthetic value and expressive potential. Symmetry conveys a feeling of stability and poise, whereas asymmetry suggests action and excitement. The balance achieved through asymmetrical structuring is less obvious and therefore tends to arouse curiosity. The felt tensions stimulate the perceiver to respond more actively.

Doris Humphrey, a gifted choreographer, understood so well the relative value of symmetry and asymmetry in spatial design. She recognized the functional role of symmetrical design in everyday life but believed that people did not always want security, comfort, and repose when they entered the world of aesthetics. Art is for stimulation, excitement, adventure. She knew that the art of movement, like other arts, needed moments of rest and repose that are often most satisfying when symmetrically designed. But, she cautioned that symmetry should be used sparingly. She believed that asymmetry, which stimulates the senses, should be understood and used more extensively in dance.[6]

The young choreographer will come to understand the use of symmetrical and asymmetrical design through experience. He should create phrases of movement that emphasize each approach to balance. Asymmetrical design probably needs more attention, since students have a natural tendency to use symmetry. Sometimes it is helpful to illustrate what happens to the expressive value of the movement when it is changed from symmetrical to asymmetrical design. Such a visual demonstration clarifies the difference in tension quality and excitement evoked by symmetry and asymmetry.

DIRECTION IN SPACE

The spatial path of action may be straight or curved, and the direction may be forward, sideward, or circular. The aesthetic potential of a movement pattern can be increased or diminished by modifying the spatial design. Each direction or path of action has a direct bearing on the expressive value of dance. Therefore the choreographer must work with a sensitive and critical eye and make aesthetic judgments about direction in terms of the intent of the dance.

Aesthetic awareness of spatial factors is acquired gradually. It requires a sensitivity that comes primarily from experiencing and feeling. This kind of experiencing, which should start early, can be incorporated with the study of movement fundamentals as well as creative problems. For example, the walk, skip, slide, and run that are natural means of traveling through space can be executed in such a way that the student will increase his sensitivity to spatial possibility as he develops fundamental

---

[6] Doris Humphrey, *The Art of Making Dances* (New York: Holt, Rinehart & Winston, Inc., 1959), p. 50.

skill. The following illustrations suggest possibilities for this kind of emphasis.

During the first stages of learning a fundamental skill such as a skip or run, the student finds it easiest to move forward in a straight path. This undeviating movement leaves him free to concentrate on such things as push-off, elevation, landing, body alignment, and transfer of weight. But as soon as he is able to control the basic elements of the skill, he is ready to modify direction and body facing. For instance, direction can be varied by moving diagonally left or right. This innovation can be followed by a combination of directions such as diagonal left, diagonal right, and directly forward. Then students may be asked to keep the sequence of directions constant but to make the changes in direction as they wish.

The result might be a combination such as three skips on the left diagonal, five on the right diagonal, and four forward. The pattern might be varied by moving sideward to the left five skips and then to the right with three skips. The same progression could be varied with a half turn on very skip. This pattern should be introduced at a moderate tempo and on a broad base with a feeling of expansiveness, and then it may be changed to a moderately fast tempo with a feeling of closeness, tightness.

The difference in the kinesthetic feel of the curved and straight path may be sensed through informal exploration with some basic movement such as a walk. For example, have students try moving about the room first in straight paths and then in curved paths. Have them continue the curved path across the floor and take circular paths to the left, followed by a circular path to the right, and continue alternating. This pattern may be modified by increasing or decreasing the dimension of the circle. Then the large and small circles may be combined.

The curved path might be modified so that it becomes a half or a semicircle instead of a complete circle. The semicircles might be performed on alternate sides on an imaginary straight line stretching across the floor. Try these as large and small areas. Add imagery to heighten the feeling aspect of the spatial pattern.

Body facings need to be experienced in relation to various paths of action. The natural body facing, at least for the beginner, is usually forward. Moving with the body facing forward can be a powerful way of relating to people, space, and objects in the stage area, but it is only one means. Other facings such as sideward and backward, create important relationships also. The kinesthetic impact of different body facings should be understood so that the individual will use them effectively in his creative work.

DIMENSION

The dimension of the movement pattern significantly affects the projection and communication of the dancer's intent. Most people have a natural tendency to move in their everyday activity with certain dimensional characteristics; therefore their dance movement tends to reflect these same characteristics. Some individuals move habitually in a small and contained manner, whereas others use large, expansive movements. Since the dimension of movement is significantly related to the spatial and dynamic aspects of dance, the choreographer must be able to move in many ways. He must be capable of moving beyond that which seems natural, if he is to achieve the full aesthetic value of dimension. The student's range of movement can be extended through experience with technique and improvisation that emphasize the dimensional aspect of movement.

Space-force relationships in the stage area

As the dancer studies his craft, he must be concerned with aspects of movement from the standpoint of balance, plane, direction, and dimension. But in order for this basic insight and skill to become functional, he must understand the use of space as it relates to the stage area. The stage is the dance arena. In this magic area the dancer creates a spatial relationship that heightens aesthetic awareness.

It is important to remember that the various areas of stage space do not exist for the perceiver until the dancer brings them into focus and defines them. The mature choreographer, knowing this, uses great care in pointing up or eliminating spatial areas and thus intensifies the aesthetic value of his work. The dance student must discover the value of the various areas of the stage and learns to use stage space with discrimination and skill.

A visual demonstration is a good means of introducing the study of stage space. Through the demonstration the dancer can discover kinesthetically as well as intellectually what happens when movement is performed with different spatial orientations. The demonstration may be presented in several ways. The following example suggests one approach.

Have students sit facing a marked-off stage area at one end of the studio. Use one of the dancers to illustrate various ways to move in the stage area and create awareness of space. Also point out the dynamic value of different uses of space.

Place the dancer at any spot to show how the observer's awareness of space is limited to the area in which the figure moves. Now shift the dancer's location to a new spot to show again that awareness of space is related to the dancer. In other words, space appears to exist when some change takes place in the environment and when something happens. The dancer's movement in the stage area is like a rock thrown into the pool. It upsets the calm and mobilizes the space.

Continue the exploration of stage space by having the dancer move in various areas to discover the relative strength of each. Compare the center areas—dead center, front, and back center—with side and corner areas. The off-center side area will appear weakest. The corner areas are stronger, but the center areas are strongest. The dead-center area has the greatest power of all. To illustrate the effect of direction of movement, have the dancer move in a straight path across the front of the stage from side to side and then across the back of the stage. Now have him move in a straight path from upstage to downstage through the center area. Have him repeat the straight path moving on various diagonals. Observers should note the way the path of movement carries the eye into space. They should also perceive the relative strength of each path. Have the dancer try moving in a curved path using small and large semicircles and reversed semicircles or scallops. Compare the curved path with the straight one. Move the group of dancers in various designs, and alternate direction and dynamics to illustrate the use of movement as a means of creating space tensions and the illusion of forces that seem to push and pull or attract and withdraw.

Dimension can be illustrated by having the dancer move first in a small rectangular pattern in center stage and then in a larger rectangular pattern that uses the full stage area. Do the same with large and small circular patterns. Go from large to small and from small to large. Have the students observe the kinesthetic effect of increasing and decreasing space area. Have the dancer improvise a two-dimensional pattern that moves from side to side; then change the improvisation to a three-dimensional study. Students should note the differences in space consumed and in their awareness of space. Have them experiment in a sitting or standing position with movement that has a feeling of expansiveness and openness. Then they might try for the opposite—a feeling of confinement and closedness. Have students observe the relationship of space design to the aesthetic intent. In contrast to dimension, they should notice how awareness of space is limited to different levels, when the action takes place near the floor, on the knees, in a standing position, with an arm stretched upward, and when the body is elevated off the floor as in a jump.

For such a demonstration to be most useful, the teacher and student should summarize the experience and identify certain ideas or principles related to the use of space. After this clarification, proceed to the next step, which is the real test of learning. Give the student a chance to apply these ideas to his own creative work. Choreograph short studies that use movement to make space come alive and support the aesthetic intent. Motivation for these studies might be the idea of confinement. The image should dictate the spatial design. Another possibility for study might be to create movement patterns, motivated by such feelings as curiosity, desperation, or apathy, that establish some relationship with a point of focus or pull between two points.

Movement can be used, of course, to create an illusion of space. The extension of an arm sidewards can carry the eye beyond the hand, and the focus of the face can create awareness of space upward, outward, downward, and at a close range or at a great distance. A dance may end with a figure moving offstage to give the illusion of traveling on and on into eternity. Such illusions do not happen as a result of a single movement, but instead emerge out of a sensitive organization of movement and space that prepares the way for the specific movement that creates the final illusion. Marcel Marceau, the renowned mime, creates space illusion with great skill. He can evoke the kinesthetic experience of climbing long winding stairs or of walking a tightrope high above the ground with movement that is confined to a small area of the stage floor.

Other motivations for creating the illusion of space are the ideas of a high precipice, a circular arena, the ferris wheel, or some distant attraction. Creative problems that emphasize the spatial illusion can be challenging.

Summary

The spatial design contributes to the clarity and meaning of dance. It is a means of attracting and holding the attention of the viewer so that he is led towards the full comprehension of the dance idea. Space is molded and made to come alive, thus creating a play of tension that is felt as a force relationship between the dancers and the environment. The felt tension evokes a kinesthetic response that makes possible the perception of meaning in the work of art.

Space, like any other element in dance, does not function in isolation. As the dancer conceives a spatial organization, rhythm and quality are inherent in the design. That is, the imaginative response to a motivation is accompanied by feelings that influence all aspects of the movement—its intensity, duration, and stress, as well as the spatial orientation. Because all aesthetic elements affect each other, the spatial design will be heightened or weakened by the rhythmic structure and the quality of movement that molds the design.

RHYTHM AS AN AESTHETIC ELEMENT

Rhythm is one of the most powerful aesthetic elements of dance. It is, at once, an organizer and a means of perceiving. As an organizer, rhythm might be thought of as a potent force that binds together the various elements of dance into a unified and harmonious structure. As a means of perceiving, the rhythm structure of the dance, with its recurring and developing patterns, provides a framework that makes for clarity and leads the viewer to an awareness of the aesthetic intent.

Every movement or series of movements possesses an internal organization of time and intensity value. Since rhythm is an inherent aspect of movement, the choreographer works simultaneously with movement and rhythm. Within a single process he designs the movement and molds the rhythmic structure of the dance phrase and eventually the total work. The creative artist recognizes rhythm as a means of strengthening tension relationships in the movement sequence and also as a means of developing continuity and dynamic flow in the dance. In other words, the rhythmic structure of movement contributes significantly to the orderliness of the dance and to its aesthetic value.

From the spectator's standpoint, rhythm is a compelling force that captures his attention and sustains his interest. Seldom will an individual fail to respond to the pulse or beat of a dance. Following this first response, which might be called the kinesthetic awareness of the underlying pulse, the observer begins to sense the repetition and progression of rhythm, as well as the accents or points of interest within the structure. When he discerns a pattern of harmonious relationship within the rhythmic structure, he is motivated to pursue the experience and usually will find it enjoyable. On the other hand, if he senses the rhythmic structure as a chaotic arrangement without form, he is apt to find the experience unpleasant and will tend to avoid it. The human being's innate tendency to seek form in all experiences causes him to seek organization and order in rhythmic structure of dance as well. It is through the process of associating and grouping isolated occurrences that he discovers meaning in choreography, or any experience. The rhythmic organization of a choreography establishes tension pulls that lead the observer towards the discovery of the meaning of dance.

Rhythm manifests itself in dance movement through muscular tension. Within every movement there is the moment of energy expenditure and the point of relaxation, or the release of tension. This action is referred to as the work-rest cycle. A repetition of any work-rest cycle sets up a rhythm. Such a cycle is demonstrated by the heartbeat, the hammering of a nail, or the tapping of a foot.

Recurring movements set in action by new expenditures of energy produce change and reveal the time element of the activity. Each recurring movement cycle exists for a specific period of time; that is, it has a duration. The duration of each movement and movement cycle is fixed in proportion to each other. The action may exist for a long or short period of time.

A series of recurring changes in movement establishes a sequence of time intervals. When these intervals are of equal length, the changes establish a steady and regular flow of energy that we identify as an *even* rhythm. When the sequence of recurring movements is made up of a combination of long and short intervals, an irregular pattern of changes is established, to which we refer as an *uneven* rhythm.

The organization of time intervals of dance movement affects the expressive value of the dance. For example, our responses to even and uneven rhythms are not the same. Usually the uneven flow, sensed as more dynamic and interesting, gives the feeling of changing and going somewhere, whereas the even rhythm, which progresses at a moderate or slow pace, tends to be restful and sometimes monotonous. The effect of the rhythmic structure of energy or feeling response is illustrated in the following line drawings:

Going someplace

Does not change

Does change

Emphasis, or stress, added at certain points in the movement structure affects the tensional relationships of the dance. Also, the pace of the total action affects the kinesthetic response, because different rates of speed alter the perception of inherent force relationships of the movement sequence and hence alter the feeling and meaning of the dance.

Obviously the rhythmic structure of a dance phrase is more complex than that of the simple work-rest cycle of nail driving, but the same principles are operative in each activity. The dance phrase is comprised of recurring and developing movements of varying durations. A unique rhythmic structure takes form as a movement phrase is created. The rhythmic structure is made up of certain groupings of pulse beats and accents that are superimposed over an underlying pulse. In other words, movements exist for varying intervals of time. They may have a short or long duration. As a result of the grouping of time intervals, an accent created by the movement, a rhythmic structure evolves. This rhythmic structure takes shape as a rhythmic phrase with its own unique internal relationship among the varying time intervals. The rhythmic phrase like the movement phrase has a sense of wholeness with a beginning and end and conveys a feeling of continuity and development.

The rhythmic organization of the total choreographic work emerges in somewhat the same manner as it does for a single dance phrase. Just as there is a final dance form that results from the manipulation and development of movement, so there is a final rhythmic form made up of rhythmic phrases and their development.

The student of dance must understand the aesthetic value of the rhythm or time element in dance. He must develop a kinesthetic awareness of tension qualities created by duration, accent, and speed, and know how to use the time element for effective organization of forces within the total dance. Our next considerations are how the student discovers the aesthetic values of the rhythmic element in dance and how he applies his knowledge to his creative work.

Rhythmic ingredients of dance

Sometimes teachers of dance have leaned on musical knowledge and principles rather than on insight about the rhythmic structure inherent in movement as a means of teaching the time element. Frequently the inexperienced dance student is asked to use the highly refined system of musical notation with its note values, measures, and phrasing before he has had a chance to discover kinesthetically the inherent rhythm of dance movement. His own dance inventions have a rhythmic structure. They are made up of movements that vary in duration, place stress at certain points, and move at a certain speed. The recurring movements establish a pattern of time intervals or rhythmic structure. Would it not be more logical for the dancer to discover the rhythmic aspects of his dance movement and to develop kinesthetic awareness and understanding of the aesthetic value of the time element in movement before the intellectual concepts and symbols of music are introduced? If the kinesthetic experience in dance does not precede, it should at least parallel the study of rhythmic elements of music.

Rhythm should be approached first through the dance experiences that lead to awareness of pulse, duration, and accent. This can be done through guided exploration and improvisation experiences that are focused on rhythmic elements of movement. An observation of a move-

ment phrase may be used as a means of introducing the rhythmic aspects
of dance structure. In this type of preview, the teacher may use a dance
study that was developed in relation to some previous dance problem.
The student may be prepared for the observation through comments
such as the following:

> *A dance is made up of a series of movements. Each movement
> exists for a certain period of time. A movement may have a long or
> short duration, depending on its motivation and purpose. As you
> look at the dance, observe the way the movement and time intervals
> are grouped. For example, there may be a series of movements that
> have a short duration followed by a movement of long duration.
> Your eyes and kinesthetic response will help you identify the time
> intervals. The vision is important, but this time you will concen-
> trate on the "feeling" of the duration. Try to feel the duration in
> your own body.*

DURATION

As soon as the student has had an opportunity to see and identify basic
rhythmic elements and to sense their effect on the feeling quality of
dance, the exploration can proceed to other experiences that emphasize
kinesthetic awareness. For example, through a simple movement of the
arm, one can experience duration. Here are a few suggestions that will
clarify this procedure:

> *Move the arm in a large circle. Then repeat several times, keeping
> the size of the circles and speed of the movements the same.*

> *Moving at the same speed, inscribe a small circle.*

> *Continue the movement and make several exact repetitions of your
> small circle. Now repeat the large circle and concentrate on the
> duration of the movement. Repeat the small circle and get the feel
> of it. Now form a large circle and a small circle alternately.*

Repeat the same pattern of circular movements using other parts of the body—leg, torso, head.

Now have students experiment with movement in a horizontal plane. They should attend to the feeling of time consumed by the movement:

Move the arms outward away from the center of the body, and then return over the same path to the starting point. Move with a feeling of largeness. Now repeat the movement out and in, keeping the movement's dimension and speed the same. Transfer the movement to another part of the body, but keep the duration the same.

Now repeat the movement with the arm at the same speed, but make the path much shorter. Transfer to another part of the body.

Combine the long and short movement of the arm.

Now, instead of regular alterations, vary the combination so that you repeat the long and short movements in different sequences. For example, you might have this pattern:

Observe improvisation of other students. Let your body feel the difference in the movement of long and short duration and the various combinations. Continue the improvisation. Work for greater contrast. Vary the length of the long duration. Make some of them very long, and then make some very short. Combine the long and short movements in various ways.

Follow the explorations such as these with a discussion of duration. Attend to the kinesthetic awareness and inner feel of the long and short durations. Use a blackboard to illustrate the relationship of various time intervals of movement.

Longer

Long

Short

Shorter

Combination

PULSE

The pulse that penetrates the movement pattern must be felt inwardly. It is not enough to rely on count. The dancer must continue to feel the pulse inside his body, regardless of the duration of movement performed. Again, an observation can be useful in bringing about kinesthetic awareness of pulse. For example, have the students observe a movement phrase and attend to the recurring pulse. As a means of externalizing the felt pulse, tap a hand or a foot. This experience can be used as a springboard for the study of meter, but at this point, the attention should be kept on pulse and duration.

It is one thing to observe and feel the pulse of movement performed by another person, and quite a different matter to work actively and accurately oneself with pulse. In order to sharpen awareness and accuracy, it may be helpful to move in relation to a steady pulse that is set by the accompanist. Use the piano or a drum. The experience may be guided in the following manner:

> *Walk in any direction, taking a step on every pulse beat. The drum continues to sound every pulse beat. Continue walking, but change the time intervals in your step. Hold some of them for longer duration, perhaps two, three, or four pulse beats. Now shorten the time interval of your step, perhaps taking two or three steps to a pulse beat. Combine long and short. Improvise over the pulse. Try various combinations of long and short intervals.*

EMPHASIS ON PULSE BEATS

Emphasis on certain pulse beats establishes accent. Have the students experiment by placing stress at different points moving informally about the room or in a diagonal path across the room:

> *Walk on every pulse beat. . . . From time to time accent the pulse beat by taking a stronger step. Then try stressing pulse beats in different ways like clapping, slapping the thigh, changing the focus of the face, or changing the direction of the walk. Through improvisation establish two or three points of accent. Keep the*

established pattern and repeat it across the floor. Observe different movement patterns. Select one or two of the patterns and show the intervals and accents diagrammatically on the blackboard.

Discuss the role of accent in establishing groupings of pulse beats and meter.

RHYTHMIC PATTERN

Concentrate on the rhythmic pattern that results from grouping time intervals and accents. Establish four pulse beats as the yardstick. The accompanist may improvise sound intervals with the time unit of four pulse beats. The class will listen to one grouping and then walk, making the change of weight repeat the exact intervals of sound. Any combination of long and short intervals may be introduced, but the introduction must occur within the yardstick of four pulse beats. As soon as the students can follow accurately, they may be encouraged to use other parts of the body more fully and to change direction and level. The game of "convert the sound to movement" might go like this:

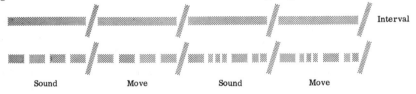

Holding one rhythmic pattern against a counter one is challenging and tests the student's ability to maintain a rhythmic structure. For example, use a three against a four. Students *A* and *B* move diagonally across the floor, stepping on every pulse beat. Student *A* groups his steps into threes, accenting the first step ('- -). Student *B* groups his steps into four, accenting the first step ('- - -). While the accompanist keeps a steady pulse beat, students *A* and *B* superimpose their own accents so that *A* is doing a three against *B*'s four. Then, instead of walking on every pulse beat, change the duration of movements within the unit of three or four, but continue to maintain the accent.

Rhythm in spoken words can be used as motivation for inventing rhythmic patterns. Any sequence of words creates a rhythm. The words may be spoken slowly or rapidly, sometimes with emphasis, other times with hesitation. They may be uttered with strength and conviction or with delicacy and caution. The rhythm created by the flow of words is influenced by the feeling and meaning that motivates the words. For instance, look at the following series of words. Read them first without any emphasis as though each word were a regular pulse beat:

Ah yes but then who knows it could be yes it could be no who is to decide tell me tell me.

Now read the words in several ways. Let the emphasis and timing be influenced by some image that causes you to respond with feeling. Consider situations that might be characterized as follows: pleasant, warm, loving; anguished, fearful; angry, distrustful; hopeful, patient.

Start with the first situation. Have students concentrate on the image and feelings about the situation. Then read the words aloud together. Do the same for the other three situations. Now have different individuals read the words aloud with their own image in mind. Note the difference in rhythmic structure.

This type of experience may be used as preparation for a creative problem that emphasizes a rhythmic pattern. Students working in small groups may be asked to make their own collection of words and use them as the source of rhythmic motivation.

Relating to music fundamentals

Up to this point, relating rhythmic elements to movement has been emphasized; but eventually the dancer must learn to count and work knowledgeably with music. After the movement phrase is created, the choreographer must understand how to translate or describe the rhythmic structure of the movement in terms of meter and formal count. This knowledge is essential for two reasons. First, the performer must be able to repeat and to maintain accuracy in the movement phrases and, second, the dancer must be able to discuss the rhythmic structure of his choreography with the composer-accompanist.

It is at this point of development that a formal knowledge of music, including meter and note value, is important. After one has developed kinesthetic awareness of rhythmic structure and has had some experience in working creatively with rhythmic factors, it is time to understand the relationship of rhythmic elements in movement to the rhythmic elements of music. An intellectual understanding of music fundamentals related to dance can be gained best in a special music class for dancers. If this type of instruction is not feasible, then music fundamentals should be included as a unit of work in the dance class. The choreographer must develop some understanding of music and learn to use music symbols, record the rhythmic structure of his dance, and communicate intelligently with the musician.

SUMMARY

From a practical standpoint, a dancer needs a keen rhythmic sense in order to perform accurately and sensitively, as well as to choreograph. He should understand the rhythmic aspects of dance and music so that he can work intelligently with the musician.

In terms of aesthetic value, rhythm plays an important role in organizing the dance movement and giving clarity to the total form. Rhythm binds together the elements of dance so that the motor forces, spatial design, and rhythmic structure result in a happening within the stage area. The unified and harmonious blending of these three elements makes action become alive and magic. The inner play of the space-time-force elements of dance creates virtual forces that are perceived as a totality or Gestalt. It is the virtual forces within the Gestalt that cause the perceiver to empathize with the dancer. The illusion created by the unified structure becomes apparent and meaningful to the perceiver through inner mimicry and experiencing of these forces.

Dance teacher works with students to build control. Photograph by William Ericson.

four

Moving with control

NATURE OF MOVEMENT

The nature and shape of movement are determined by the motivation that causes the impulse for action. The organism is stimulated to move by needs and desires that are related to the maintenance of self. Sometimes the movement is utilitarian in nature, whereas at other times movement is related solely to aesthetic needs. Examples of every day utilitarian movements, or uses of physical force to achieve a specific task, are driving a nail, lifting a book, or pushing a car.

In dance, movement is used for expressive and aesthetic purposes, although its physical properties are the same as those of utilitarian movement. The differences between aesthetic and utilitarian movement lie in the motivations that set the action in process and in the emotional tones that surround the action. One might say that motivation is a source of movement and that the nature and function of movement are determined by the felt needs and goals that spark the motivation.

The motivations that lead to dance arise from sensory experiences and feeling responses. We know that movement as the material of dance occurs because of the physical force created by exerted energy. We know also that this movement becomes dance because it is impregnated with

63

abstracted feelings that take an expressive form. The dancer is concerned with evoking an aesthetic response.

Dance as an art is both physical and emotional. These two aspects of dance are interwoven and never exist in isolation. Physical movement is transformed so that it creates an illusion of feeling state. It possesses a magic that is quite different from the utilitarian activity of everyday life.

The material of dance movement is a product of man's creative instincts. The dancer is not convincing when he moves in a mechanical and imitative manner. Only as he moves with full awareness will his movements convey sincerity and conviction. If a dancer is to produce an honest projection of images and feelings, he must have the ability to control each subtle shading of movement. He must, in fact, transform movement in such a way that the dance takes on a magic quality. To achieve this end, the dancer must have some understanding of the physical laws that control movement, as well as the imaginative and the emotional aspects of dance.

MOVEMENT PRINCIPLES

Such mundane factors as energy, gravity, and balance compensation principles are fundamentally related to the aesthetic world of dance. An understanding of these basic concepts frees the creator to control and mold movement in his own image.

Energy-force principle

Before the human body or any of its parts can move in any way, there must be an expenditure of energy and application of force. As a result of an impulse, energy is released, muscles and levers are set in action, and movement is accomplished. The duration, intensity, and speed of each movement are determined by the amount of energy and the degree of force. The output of energy is directly related to the motivation and the strength of the emotional stimulus. Following the depletion of the initial period of energy output or effort, there is a concluding phase of relaxation or rest. Sometimes we refer to these as the tension and release phases of movement.

The energy-force phenomenon can be illustrated very simply with movement of the arm. While standing in a comfortable stride position, trunk bent forward with left hand on the left knee, let the right arm hang loosely from the shoulders. If the arm is relaxed it will dangle, perhaps with a slight swinging action at first; but soon it becomes quite motionless and will remain in that position until an impulse causes new action. When you are ready, expend a little energy (give a little push) in any direction and then let the arm go on its own. The arm will move in some direction, and then, after the force is spent, the arm will drop back to the dangling position. Now try sending the arm in different directions and try using various amounts of force. Sometimes apply a great amount of force and sometimes very little.

This simple demonstration shows that the arm moves when force is applied, and only then. It illustrates also that force causes the arm to travel in some direction at some rate of speed. As long as force is applied, the arm will stay in motion, but as soon as the energy is dissipated, the arm drops back to the center. One must exert effort in order to move. The range, intensity, duration, and speed of every movement are dependent on the output of energy and force exerted.

Explorations such as the one described can further the student's understanding of basic movement concepts. In order to get the most from this kind of experience, the learner should concentrate on what is happening and attend to the accompanying sense of tension and feeling state of each phase of the action. In so doing, his knowledge of the physical laws of movement and kinesthetic awareness of movement will become more functional and, thus, enable him to control his dance material.

Gravity-balance principle

The dancer must contend at all times with a second kind of force that we know as gravity. As soon as the force exerted by the individual is spent, gravity takes over. That explains why, in the previous example, the arm always drops back to the center dangling position after the force has dissipated.

The human organism is in constant motion. This means that the body instrument is involved in a never-ending process of adjusting balance and counteracting the pull of gravity in order to maintain desired positions. Man orients himself to his position in space by identifying with the vertical and horizontal planes. When standing or moving in a vertical plane, he must maintain a balanced body to counteract the pull of gravity. When an individual lies down, gravity takes over, and the problem of balance and counteraction is diminished. Each movement between the vertical and the horizontal planes creates a new balancing situation.

This gravity principle and its relationship to movement was the basis of Doris Humphrey's theory of motion around which she built her dance. She believed that the very core of movement was to be found in the process of giving in to or rebounding from gravity. For her, all life seemed to fluctuate between two points, which she identified as the vertical and the horizontal—or life and death.[1]

The task of finding and maintaining an effective balance while in an erect vertical position should be one of the first concerns of a dance student. This is true, not because the vertical body position is the primary or most important position, but because it is the anchor point from which one orients himself to space. It is also the position from which he deviates to achieve exciting kinesthetic movement.

The human body is made up of many movable parts that include the head, neck, spine, trunk, shoulder girdle, arms, legs, and feet. Muscles, in a constant state of tension, keep the body parts in a vertical position. If body parts are properly balanced, energy is used efficiently; if poorly balanced, energy is wasted. An erect posture that allows the individual to move freely and efficiently with the least expenditure of energy is dependent on proper alignment. The movable parts of the body should be so related that the pull of gravity is directly downward through the supporting structure, or so related that the center of gravity is over the supporting base.

> Gravity may be thought of as a strong pulling force which draws all mate-
> rial objects vertically downward toward the center of the earth, holding
> them in contact with the earth's surface or with some other solid which in
> turn is in contact with the earth's surface. This force acts on all parts of
> every object, but it operates in such a way that, for practical purposes, it
> may be considered as concentrating its pull on the weight center of the
> object. The weight center is called *center of gravity*. The line that falls
> vertically downward from the center to the earth's center is called the *line
> of gravity*.[2]

The center of gravity in the human body is located in the region of the pelvis. The legs are the supporting structure for the center of gravity, and the feet are the supporting base. The problem then is to have each movable part supported one above the other so that the center line of gravity and the pull of gravity are through the legs and feet. When the body segments are properly aligned and balanced, the line of gravity, as seen from the side, passes just behind the ear, through the shoulder, the middle of the hip, and continues in front of the ankle and through the foot.

---

[1] Doris Humphrey, *The Art of Making Dances* (New York: Holt, Rinehart & Winston, Inc., 1959), p. 106.

[2] Eleanor Metheny, *Body Dynamics* (New York: McGraw-Hill Book Company, Inc., 1952), p. 98.

How does one locate and feel this alignment in his own body? Start with the feet, which are slightly apart with the weight distributed on the outer border and metatarsal bone. The knees are relaxed, the pelvic girdle is neither tilted forward nor backward but is balanced, and the rib cage is held high. The shoulders are relaxed and low. The head is well balanced on the shoulder girdle and carried high, as though being suspended from something that is directly above the center of the head. Balanced alignment, which is the starting point for movement that is efficient and economical, must be kinesthetically perceived and practiced until it becomes habitual. Then and only then does the balanced instrument become functional.

As Martha Graham has stated,

> . . . posture is dynamic, not static. It is a self portrait of being. It is psychological as well as physiological. I use the word "posture" to mean that instant of seeming stillness when the body is poised for the most intense, most subtle action, the body at its moment of greatest potential efficiency.[3]

After the dancer has learned to control alignment and balance with the weight supported over both feet, he should try shifting the weight so that the center line of gravity falls through one foot, which provides a smaller base for support. The balancing of body parts and alignment should not change. Experiment first by making a slight shift sideward, forward, and backward, and then try shifting farther away from the original center by taking larger steps.

Maintaining proper alignment of the body parts while executing movement that progresses through space on a constantly shifting base, such as a walk, run, or skip, is more difficult than shifting the center line of gravity from one foot to the other in a standing position. As the movement shifts farther away from the center, for example in a long run or full leap, greater adjustment must be made, and thus greater control is required to maintain the center and stable position.

Students enjoy large, vigorous movements and will tend to rush toward these full movements. Most people, however, achieve success more quickly in large movement if they start with smaller strides and gradually work for a full range of movement. The reason for this is obvious: accuracy of alignment can be maintained more easily when one shifts a short distance away from the original center.

During the early stage of learning, accuracy of alignment and balancing is more important than distance. Each new adjustment in space should be made with accuracy and full kinesthetic perception of the position. In this way, the individual progresses steadily in his ability to

3 Martha Graham, "A Dancer's Primer for Action," in *Dance*, ed. Frederick R. Rogers (New York: The Macmillan Company, 1941), p. 181.

control the body, and eventually he will be able to cover great distances with accuracy and efficiency. Movement that requires balancing should not be learned by chance or accident. The action must be consciously understood and kinesthetically perceived. When skills are developed in this way, they can be repeated again and again with the same effectiveness.

Sometimes dancers mistakenly think that care need only be given to alignment and balance in complicated movement rather than in all movement. This attitude is illustrated by the fact that most beginners do not know how to execute a simple dance run accurately or efficiently.

The learning of all movement skill involves understandings and kinesthetic awareness. For example, the successful execution of a simple dance run requires insight into the control of the body instrument. We cannot assume that skill in shifting the center line of gravity in the standing position will guarantee control of alignment on a moving base.

Let us look at certain problems that the beginner has with the dance run. Usually he has a tendency to move with fairly long strides and has difficulty in holding the body together. Everything seems to fall apart. First of all, the feet are not used correctly. We say, "He runs flatfooted." Then the center line of gravity is not transferred over the base of support, and, in fact, the different parts of the body all seem to be moving in different directions. The inexperienced student must learn how to maintain the efficient balancing of body parts on a moving base as well as on a stationary base.

Skill in moving through space, demanding a constant shifting of weight, is developed through experience based on a sound progression. For example, the dance run may be approached through the following types of progression:

1. Move across the floor using a prancing action. Concentrate on accurate push-offs and landing action.

2. Continue the prancing movement, but with slightly increased strides, which creates the need for shifting of weight farther forward. Keep the emphasis on maintaining alignment, allowing no breaks in the body and sensing the shifting action.

3. Increase the push-off and stride so that the action becomes an easy run. Keep the strides small so that the correct action of the feet and transfer of weight will be continued. Carry the arms in a sideward position to avoid the coordination problem.

4. Sometimes it is useful to combine the prancing and easy running to develop kinesthetic awareness of alignment in the vertical and the

leaning positions. For example, four prances in vertical position followed by four runs in forward leaning position would increase awareness of needed adjustment.

5. As control of this action on the moving base is gained, continue the run and gradually increase the stride. A sudden lunging forward tends to destroy all that has been gained.

6. Now arm movement should be added. Arms should move in opposition to the legs and should swing forward and backward in an easy manner. This action requires coordination and also makes necessary the controlled movement of the shoulders, which should remain low and in place as the arm swings forward.

7. From this point of development it is possible to modify the movement by changing direction, rhythmic pattern, tempo, or body facing. Running backward requires a new emphasis on elevation, because some elevation is necessary in order to get full leg extension. Also, moving backward necessitates a new adjustment in weight shifting. Eventually, the run must be combined with other movement and controlled in patterns that make different uses of the spatial, rhythmic, and dynamic dimensions.

Speed is another factor that affects alignment or balancing of body parts. If one moves too rapidly in the early stages of learning, speed tends to destroy accuracy. Action takes place so fast that there is not time to make necessary adjustments, and more attention is given to speed than to alignment. Speed, then, as well as distance, should be increased as the individual is able to adjust the body part and control the balance with accuracy. This caution about speed relates to increase of speed beyond the medium or normal tempo.

Caution, however, does not imply that the dancer should slow down action below the normal tempo. Sometimes it is helpful to slow down in order to concentrate on some specific aspect of the movement. But slow motion should be practiced only for brief periods of analysis and clarification, because, as a general rule, learning takes place more readily when activity is performed at its regular or nearly regular speed. Normal tempo makes it possible to perceive the activity in its totality and to see and feel proper relationships.

Balance-compensation principle

The dancer will not be satisfied long if he relies only on movement in the vertical plane. He will soon discover that many of his motivations spring from images and feelings that cry out for movement that is precariously balanced and irregularly shaped. The intuitively formed movement that flows from sensory experience may assume a shape that requires the body part to be shifted away from the center line of gravity. For example, the hips may be thrust far to one side, the pelvic girdle may be moved backward, or the rib cage pushed sidewards. Such positions result from the force relationships inherent in the imagery. Also, the dancer uses these positions to establish tension that causes the observer to empathize and respond with kinesthetic awareness. The observer knows, as does the dancer, that when parts of the body are shifted off center, there is an immediate feeling of suspense and tension.

Within this play of gravity is the ever present danger of falling. The only way to avoid falling is to compensate or counteract the pull of gravity by moving another part of the body in an opposite direction, thus establishing a new balance. Tension must be maintained in order to keep these parts in balance. The farther off center, the greater is the tension. For example, if the hips are thrust to one side, the torso and head may be moved to the opposite side in order to establish balance. Or, if the pelvic girdle is moved backwards as though being pulled, the body will fall backward unless the trunk is bent forward enough to compensate for the displacement of weight. The principle is simply that whenever a body part moves from the line of gravity, an opposing part moves in the opposite direction so that balance is stabilized.[4]

Since the dancer must not be restricted to movement in the vertical plane, it is important that he understand the principle of compensation and also that he acquire a keen kinesthetic perception of balancing when weights are shifted off center. With this understanding, he has the freedom to move in endless ways.

As stated previously, learning skills through concept and principle is very different from learning through imitation. When the student imitates an off-center position demonstrated by the teacher, he has not learned about compensation. In a situation that calls for seeing and imitating the student learns one movement pattern. Learning principles opens the way to hundreds of movement patterns and makes it possible to achieve these movements with an economy of effort and time. The body instrument and movement material is made functional for the imaginative work in dance when man's creative spirit is working with a high degree of consciousness and kinesthetic awareness.

[4] Mary Ellen Weber, "Development of a Conceptual Model of Human Movement from Endocrine and Perceptual Theory with Analysis of the Effects of Aberrations of Movement" (Doctoral dissertation, University of California), p. 56.

MOVEMENT POTENTIAL OF THE INSTRUMENT

The many segments of the body are connected by ligaments and muscles, which make possible a great variety of motion. The joints are so constructed that they are capable of flexion, a decreasing of the angle; extension, increasing of the angle; rotation, turning on an axis; abduction, moving away from the center of the body; and adduction, moving toward the body. Every movement made by any part of the body has direction, range, speed, and quality. For example, the direction may be forward, backward, sideward, around, up, or down. The range may be small to large, the duration short to long, the speed slow to fast, and the quality tensed or relaxed. Each of these movement possibilities has many shadings determined by the amount of energy expended and the way the force is applied. The dancer must become skillful in manipulating movement and controlling the tension force, if the movement is to be used successfully as dance material.

Movement of the torso

To discover the expressive power of the torso, the dancer must explore the various movement possibilities of the body area and learn to control action in a great variety of ways. Every exploration, even the most technical, should heighten kinesthetic awareness. As a foundation for expressive use of the torso, the dancer needs the knowledge of certain structural relationships and basic movement possibilities. Since the relationship of the various parts of the skeletal framework affect the efficiency of movement, let us discuss the torso structure first.

We are concerned with the spine, shoulder, and pelvic girdle. The shoulder should be pulled down, with the neck fully extended and exposed. One should feel as though the spine is pushing through the shoulder girdle and rising above it, not hanging below. The extended spine should not alter the normal position of the pelvic girdle. The lower back normally has a slight curve, which should not be increased or flattened by the spine action.

The beginning dancer usually finds it easiest to discover and establish these proper relationships through movement experience. Action accompanied by explanation is more effective than words alone. The main purpose of such exploration should be to help the individual develop kinesthetic awareness of proper relationships so that he can control, with a minimum of effort, the desired body position.

The first exploration of a structural relationship might be made lying on the back, which eliminates the problem of gravity. The individual is free to stretch and adjust positions without encountering the gravity force. The sitting position, with legs crossed and arms extended upward, also might be used. In this position there is freedom to stretch and adjust the shoulder girdle without disturbing the lumbar area. For example, stretch the spine and arms upward, and then, while keeping the spine extended, pull the shoulders low. This is a good way to acquire the kinesthetic feel of correct shoulder positions.

Standing position is the most demanding because of the pull of gravity. In this position it is necessary to stabilize the pelvic girdle in order to avoid abnormal tilting forward or backward. The ability to assume proper structural relationship is the starting point of good movement. It provides a home base or functional framework from which the dancer can proceed to experimentation that is more demanding.

The potential movement of the torso includes flexion, extension, rotation, abduction, and adduction. Each type of action can be modified so that there are many possibilities for different movement patterns. The dancer's problem is twofold: (1) to discover the movement potential of the torso and become skillful in controlling its actions; and (2) to learn to modify the basic movement—spatially, rhythmically, and dynamically —in order to create fresh, imaginative movement needed for expressive purposes.

The dance student must learn to use the spine freely in flexion, extension, and rotation movement. Extension can occur all at once or sequentially with one part following another. It can have a range that is small or large, a speed that is fast or slow, and a quality that is tensed or relaxed. Flexion and extension of the spine may be achieved in different positions: lying, sitting, kneeling, and standing. The spine can rotate as it is kept in extended position, or it can rotate during the action of flexion or extension. The rotation action makes it possible to modify direction not only sideward and around, but also sideward upward and sideward downward.

Further modification of movement can be achieved through abduction or adduction of the shoulders. Therefore the dancer must study the flexion, extension, and rotation movements of the torso through a great variety of explorations. He must (1) discover the amazing number of movement possibilities of the torso; (2) experience expressive potential of various ways of moving; and (3) acquire the ability to control the torso action so that movement is purposeful.

This learning process is not served best by the repetition of a few so-called flexion-extension techniques. Control and accuracy in one specific technique does not necessarily guarantee good performance in other movement situations. Nor does concentration on isolated techniques develop expressive potential of the torso. If the goal of the movement or technique is to serve the expressive powers of the individual, then these experiences, even the early ones, need to be seen in relation to the ultimate goal.

Frequently young teachers frantically write down every new technique that they learn in a summer session or master class. These techniques will then be added to their repertoires. The new technique may be a very good one, but the additive process of acquiring techniques is not the real answer to good teaching and to development of young dancers. There is nothing wrong with using these set patterns, but they must be the means and not the end.

There are probably a dozen good approaches to a specific technique, and the teacher cannot use all of them. Rather than teaching all the techniques you know, have a clear focus in your approach to students. Focus on some kind of movement, such as flexion, extension, rotation of the spine, or abduction and adduction of the shoulders. When the teacher has a specific goal in mind, she can approach the movement experience in various ways—through exploration or improvisation that culminates in a structured pattern, or through the set movement pattern or technique. The crucial consideration is that the student experience basic action and come to know the principles involved. Sometimes the teacher may choose to return again and again to a certain movement pattern in order to improve accuracy and control. But when this repetition occurs, the teacher should make sure that the student's understanding of the specific, such as a rotation of the spine, is not restricted to one or two set patterns. The precise performance of the specific should be accompanied by varied experiences that require rotation in the torso through modified use of space, direction, rhythm, and dynamics. The persistent goal for the student should be not to mimic the teacher in a specific technique, but to understand his movement potential, to discover the rich resources of dance material, and to become skillful in using his body instrument to serve his creative purpose.

Movement of the extremities

The arms, legs, and head may be thought of as extensions of the torso. Movement of these parts may work with or against the action of the torso, and it may precede or follow the torso movement. In each instance there must exist a tensional relationship between the extremity and the torso or center of the body. The action often seems to start in the center and then flow through the extremity. But even when the impulse starts the action in the extremity, say in a hand, there is an inner awareness of the movement and a felt tensional relationship between the hand and the torso. A heightened kinesthetic awareness in the dancer is significantly related to expressive value of his work.

The dancer must learn to use his body instrument as an integrated whole. He must have many experiences that allow him to use the arms and legs in relation to other body parts. Movement that combines the action of extremities such as arms and legs requires greater emphasis on balance and coordination. Some people find it difficult to coordinate the movement of the arms and legs, that is, to swing the arms in opposition to the legs. Also, the minute the arms begin to move, it is more difficult to maintain the correct relationship of shoulder girdle to the spine. The shoulders tend to hunch and to move forward with an arm. Then there is the problem of experiencing the spatial relationship of the arm to the body so that a true kinesthetic awareness of the arm position is acquired. This kinesthetic awareness is important because the dancer must be able to arrive at a specific position with immediacy and accuracy.

In the use of the legs, some students encounter the problem of moving from the hip rather than the knee and of maintaining a flow of tension that conveys the integral relationship of the leg and torso. Some students have difficulty extending the leg in a straight path and tend to swing it across the body. Kinesthetic awareness of the desired spatial relationship will contribute to the achievement of accurate control.

The action of the leg makes possible progressing on a moving base as well as working on a stationary base. When one progresses through space, movement assumes a new dimension and expressive potential. With the new potential come the problems of maintaining balance and timing and of achieving coordination. In a sense the moving base is a testing ground. Can the newly learned movement skills be performed effectively on a moving base? Movement skills do not transfer automatically to the moving base, because they require new adjustments, particularly in relation to gravity and balance. Therefore students must have the opportunity to transpose newly learned movement and principles from the stationary base to the movement base.

Usually it is wise to keep the early moving experiences simple so that the focus of the learner can be on the relationship of body parts, correct action, and timing. Basic locomotive patterns such as slides, skips, runs, and walks are good starting points. As the student develops control, the movement pattern may become more complex and may be modified spatially, rhythmically, and dynamically.

The teacher and the student should be aware of the total movement

'Fractional Assemblies" performed by Ronald Brown and Angelica Leung of the UCLA Dance Company, 1987. Photograph by Becky Villaseñor.

pattern and body action, but within this wholeness there should be a point of emphasis. Although the beginning student may be able to keep a general feeling of the whole movement and, at the same time, concentrate on one or two specific points, he is apt to become frustrated if he is asked to think of too many specific things. Therefore, within the larger framework of the whole movement pattern, the teacher should shift the focus of attention from time to time and bring about the gradual increase of confidence in all areas. Here again the emphasized aspect of the movement should be stressed as the student is ready for that emphasis. The part that is emphasized should always be seen in relation to the whole movement.

The sequence of these basic movement experiences cannot be predetermined. The order and specific emphasis must take shape in relation to the student's development. However, there are certain areas of development that are fundamental and usually follow in somewhat the same order. Certainly some degree of accuracy in basic movements and relationships of body parts is fundamental. For example, in the elementary skip, slide, or run there is need to concentrate on correct foot action—the push-off, landing, and toeing straight ahead. The path of the leg swing should also be observed. Does it swing straight forward or backward, or does it swing outward or across? The teacher must observe the shifting of the center line of gravity on the progressively shifting base. Is the weight centered over each new step? The tendency of many beginners is to keep the weight too far back so that they reduce the efficiency of the movement. This error may be checked by stopping them in midaction or by having students observe each other.

The torso and legs must be related, and finally, the action of an integrated body—arms, torso, and legs—must be achieved. The ultimate goal is to move through space with torso lifted, arms swinging easily, shoulders held low, while the feet and legs perform accurately. In other words, the alignment is controlled and all parts are used accurately as the weight is shifted with rhythmic accuracy.

As soon as the student has some degree of security with the basic locomotive pattern, he should begin to explore more fully the use of direction, body facing, and rhythm. Besides forward and backward, he should move sideward, diagonally, and around. He should experience moving in various directions with the body facing forward, backward, and sideward. Rhythmic patterns should be varied and gradually become more complex. Tempos should vary from slow to fast.

Early locomotor experiences are usually done with a stabilized torso; that is, the shoulder girdle, spine, and pelvic girdle are kept in normal relationship. This type of control is fundamental to locomotor activity.

But after the dancer has developed skill in moving with the normally aligned body, he will want to modify the action of the upper body and produce new coordination of the torso, arms, and head on a rhythmic moving base.

To achieve variations the dancer should explore movement of the torso involving flexion, extension, rotation, abduction, or adduction. The action of the upper body may occur on various planes ranging between the vertical and the horizontal and may sometimes occur with body weights off center. Obviously the coordination, balance, and timing problems are greater in this type of movement. As the individual discovers and learns to handle this kind of movement, he will want to use it in his creative work.

Quality of movement should be emphasized in early experiences rather than adding it after skill has been developed. Motivation and quality of movement should be integrated in basic dance experiences. To achieve this integration, the movement pattern may evolve from a motivation, or imagery may be related to a specific movement sequence.

ADEQUACY OF THE INSTRUMENT

As the student progresses creatively and intellectually, he has increasing need for an instrument that will perform fluently and accurately. Discovery of movement possibilities and understanding of the basic movement principles provide only a partial foundation for dance. To achieve movement possibilities, the instrument must be strong and pliable. Since successful dance movement requires a much greater range of motion than is used in daily life, the dancer must work to increase *flexibility* of the joints—ankle, hip, spine, and shoulder. To increase range of motion, one must work beyond the usual range.

Accurate performance depends on strength. The muscle structure must be strong enough to thrust the body into space, control movement with sureness, and sustain an activity over a period of time. To increase strength, the muscle groups must be used actively and pushed beyond their usual activity by increasing the load or the speed.

The capacity to sustain activity over an extended period of time requires endurance. For example, the leg muscles must be strong enough to allow the dancer to repeat the jump for the desired number of times, and the heart muscle must be strong enough to allow him to move through space with full speed and efficiency. To increase endurance, the dancer must push beyond the usual demand and continue work for successively longer periods before stopping.

Adequacy in the areas of flexibility, strength, and endurance contribute to the adequacy of the instrument and thus to the creative freedom of the individual. Although these developmental aspects of movement cannot be ignored, they should not be given undue emphasis. They are means to an end and are valuable only as they further the total dance experience. Sometimes we unfortunately hear students discuss dance in terms of flexibility exercises. Such a concept of dance is apt to prevail when the emphasis is on exercises rather than dance as a creative experience. A student should work on flexibility with the knowledge that he needs a greater range of movement in order to work creatively and to perform more freely. Work in the areas of flexibility, strength, and endurance should start early and continue as long as the individual dances, and these developmental experiences should be integrated within the larger context of dance.

KINESTHETIC AWARENESS AND CONTROL

The acquisition of dance skills and the ability to repeat specific movements with fluency is dependent on kinesthetic perception. In order to move beautifully and efficiently, the individual must develop the "feel" of rightness or wrongness. This feel or kinesthetic sense enables him to assume a specific position or perform with accuracy a certain movement pattern that requires balance and adjustment of spatial relationships of the body part.

Kinesthetic perception is a result of an awareness of sensory data. By means of receptors located in the muscles, tendons, and joints, we feel the muscle tension and body position of a specific movement. The awareness of the muscle tension inherent in a correct or desired position makes it possible to re-establish the same movement with a minimum of effort.

As pointed out in the previously cited work of Weber,[5] there is increasing evidence that kinesthetic perception is a result of an aggregate or synthesis of sensory data and therefore involves more than the muscle sense. Some of the research in the area of perception indicates that visual sensory data of spatial orientation of the body and rhythmic sensations of time intervals of the movement are important ingredients in the kinesthetic sense. In other words, the sensory information resulting from muscle tension and spatial and temporal orientation are integrated into a synthesized sensation that results in a kinesthetic perception.

Since kinesthetic perception is related to motor learning, it is im-

---

[5] Weber, "Development of a Conceptual Model of Human Movement from Endocrine and Perceptual Theory with Analysis of the Effects of Aberrations of Movement," p. 75.

portant that the dancer attend to the feeling sensation of the movement. Reliance on a mechanical performance is not sufficient. The learner should search out the sensation surrounding each movement pattern so that he will develop a keen awareness of sensory data. Emphasis on perception of the movement experience ensures economy of learning and greater control with less effort.

MOVEMENT "ALIVENESS"

The dancer speaks through the integrated totality of movement, not through separate body parts. His concern with parts should always be directed towards the improved functioning of the total body instrument. This means that as he increases his skill and control of the parts of the body, he must at the same time learn to move with the total body awareness.

This so-called total body awareness or "aliveness" is a curious thing. Although every true dancer knows exactly what the term means and talks freely about the total organism's being related actively to dance and about the inner tension that is maintained throughout the dance, still it is nearly impossible to define this state. Perhaps the condition of total awareness can be described best as a feeling state produced by associated tension in which the total organism is actively absorbed. It exists with the opening of the dance and is not released, not even for a minute, until the end of the dance. An inner awareness surrounds and penetrates each movement, even the smallest one. It is this "something" that sparks the observer, sets up tensions within his body, and causes him to respond kinesthetically. Without it the observer is unmoved.

How does the student acquire this rather mysterious quality of the dance? Certainly it cannot be conveyed through verbal explanation or any other method. All the teacher can hope to do is to help each individual discover and develop his own sensitivity.

The dancer talks about movement emanating from the center and identifies the middle of the torso as the center. He is not thinking of this spot as a center of gravity but rather as a center or source of energy and feeling. Isadora Duncan referred to this center as the soul. Today we do not speak of the soul, but we are concerned with the center for several reasons. From a structural point of view, the torso is central. We certainly would not think of an arm or leg as being the center of a body structure, but instead we think of them as appendages extending from the torso. This fact in itself would seem to justify the idea of movement flowing from the torso. The dancer, however, takes this fact for granted and is more concerned with the organicism of the movement and its power to convey the images and feelings of man.

Perhaps the explanation of the center as the source of movement aliveness is that the life sustaining organs—the lung, heart, viscera—reside in the torso area. The middle of the body seems to be the spot where one feels the first reaction of emotional experiences, such as anguish, fear, or pleasure. We say that something has hit us "right in the middle," or "in the pit of our stomachs."

Doris Humphrey believed that students should become aware of this feeling center through exploration of the natural sources of emotion. According to her,

> . . . Deeply felt emotions always begin in the middle of the body, where the heart, lungs, and the viscera respond immediately and first. Other reactions may follow very swiftly, so as to seem simultaneous—the hands may fly to any of those parts or to the head, or be clasped close to the body, and so forth. Also, reactions of the head, legs, and other parts of the body may follow. These would depend on the nature of the feeling. If it is a sudden shock, the hands will go to the breast or heart where an immediate, violent increase of tension is going on; or to the head, or to the eyes, if the emotion involves a wish to shut out the painful sensation, or if weeping is indicated. If this feeling is not sharp, like a shock, the gradual realization, reaction, will still come first in the middle of the body as always, but may be accompanied by more peripheral movement, such as rollings and liftings of the head, clasping or beating of the hands against some outside object or restless movement of the feet.[6]

These movement responses, of course, are not the final dance material, but as Miss Humphrey has stated, they are related to the feeling source that motivates honest and convincing movement.

Moving-breathing relationships

No doubt the aliveness of movement is related to breathing. The feeling center we have been discussing is also the location of the mechanism that controls breathing, and the cycle of inhalation and exhalation is the very essence of life. The dancer, very much aware of moving in relation to breathing, knows that each movement must be filled with breath if it is to be "alive." The layman would think it very strange to talk about filling the arms and legs with breath, but not so the dancer.

Doris Humphrey knew the kinesthetic value of movement-breath relationships and included the idea of breath rhythm in her movement theory based on "giving into" and "rebounding from" gravity. Emphasizing the breath relationship to movement, she has said,

---

6 Humphrey, *The Art of Making Dances*, p. 112.

In the dance we can use a simple rise and fall of breath in its original location in the chest, but this is by no means all. The idea of breath rhythm —the inhalation, the suspension, and the exhalation—can be transferred to other parts of the body. One can "breathe" with the knees, or the arms, or the whole body. This transference will not seem artificial, but miraculously natural and satisfying.[7]

What, then, does this center for feeling and breathing have to do with moving with control? The answer lies in the fact that the dancer is always trying to control movement so that it will serve aesthetic and expressive purposes. Of course, he must be concerned with structural considerations and developmental techniques, but never as ends in themselves. Movement should always be related functionally to the expressive and communicative purposes that it is supposed to serve. This end can be achieved best when the dancer possesses a high degree of kinesthetic awareness in the torso area. This kinesthetic awareness can make movement appear to originate and flow from the body center, or to have an integral relationship with the center.

SUMMARY

Obviously the dancer must discover certain norms in balance and movement, explore movement possibilities, and learn basic principles that govern efficient movement. He must develop a heightened kinesthetic awareness, and he must become skillful in manipulating movement in such a way that it reveals his images. But, as Martin says,

> He not only needs to know how to play his instrument, but he must also build it out of himself, and keep it tuned at all times.[8]

The phrase "build it out of himself" is important to this discussion. It is so easy and, in fact, is such a temptation for the teacher and the student to get carried away with the aspects of the movement that may contribute to a fine technician but not necessarily to a dancer.

Doris Humphrey said about the dancer's technique,

> If it is in the service of nothing, nothing will result except the awareness that everybody has technique. Technicians are a dime a dozen. . . . Something must be added to make this display worthwhile and that something is motivation.[9]
>
> . . . One of the most notable effects of motivation in movement is the power to coordinate. The dancer, when he is really suffused with feeling of

---

[7] Humphrey, *The Art of Making Dances*, p. 107.

[8] John Martin, "Isadora Duncan and Basic Dance," in *Isadora Duncan*, ed. Paul Magrill (New York: Holt, Rinehart & Winston, Inc., 1947), p. 12.

[9] Humphrey, *The Art of Making Dances*, p. 110.

which he understands most of the import, will be "all of a piece." That is, no one part of the body will be out of line, so as to make it necessary to control or alter it by a conscious effort. This is a great saving of energy, but it will happen only if the dancer is able to find the real roots of the emotional behavior and wrap himself in them.[10]

Relating the motivational and the technical aspects of the dance is one of the greatest problems of the dance teacher. We have not been sure about how to approach creative dance, and all too often the dance experience has remained at the technical level. Some people were aware of the need for teaching dance as a creative art experience even in the early developments of contemporary dance. Why is it that only in recent years we have made significant progress in the creative aspects of dance?

In 1947 Martin said about the teaching of dance,

The dancer's habit of moving must be made such that the movement is never an end in itself, but always the ultimate result of an inward awareness. . . . The dancer must be trained neither to make somebody else's movement, nor to resort to mechanically contrived routines, but, quite the contrary, every ounce of his energy must be directed to the paths of moving in his own highly personal and essentially unique manner.[11]

These comments were made by Martin at a time when teachers all across the country were placing great emphasis on imitation of techniques learned from the professional artists in dance.

What are some of the implications for teaching today? To teach dance as a whole and to avoid the devisive approach that separates the motivational and technical aspects, these basic guides seem applicable:

1. The dancer's movement experience should be vital. It should not become routinized. The set movement patterns or techniques that are used to achieve specific goals, such as extension of the back or balancing in an off-center position, should be related to some concept or principle that can be applied in many situations. In fact, the learner must have ample opportunity to apply his specific learning to other situations, either through improvisation or some other approach. The focus should be on understanding and skill in using understanding. New skills must be linked to the whole concept of dance.

2. Every movement should be imbued with an emotional tone. Since the dance situation is not a physical fitness class, movement should not be mechanical exercise. Even a movement designed to increase flexibility should be performed with sensitiveness and quality. If the dancer is concerned with expressive movement, then he must develop his own

---

[10] Humphrey, *The Art of Making Dances,* p. 114.

[11] Martin, "Isadora Duncan and Basic Dance," in *Isadora Duncan,* ed. Magrill, p. 14.

sensitivity before he will be successful in projecting qualities that will evoke an empathetic response from his audience.

3. Movement designed to further technical discipline must still contribute to freedom and spontaneity of movement. The student should be encouraged to apply to his own creative effort the newly acquired control of some specific. As he practices the discipline with spontaneity, he further develops his own unique style and form of expression. The truly creative situation does not bring forth a group of students who move in the same manner and look like carbon copies of the teacher. Only as the individual is free to respond in his own way and to be aware of self, can he find his unique expression and avoid becoming a part of a mass product.

4. Dance movement, even technique, should be performed with a sense of motivation. Although all movements are not necessarily related to a specific motivation, each dance movement should be performed sensitively and with quality. Use of motivation can help to bridge the gap between the mechanical and the aesthetic aspects of dance. Through motivated movement the dancer can discover the feeling center of his instrument and thus develop a kinesthetic awareness that helps him achieve integrated movement.

The aliveness of each movement depends on the dancer's depth of perception and feeling. Effective motivation is probably the key to creative teaching. If the ultimate goal of the dance student is to create mature, motivated works of art, then it seems logical that this relationship between motivation and movement should permeate the entire dance experience. Otherwise, how is the young artist to learn how to use movement as aesthetic material?

A sculptural effect is achieved by the position of the dancers and through dramatic lighting. Photograph by Phil Paviger.

five

Creating with form

CHOREOGRAPHING—A CREATIVE ACT

Bringing a new dance into being is truly a creative act. During the process the creator penetrates the depths of self as he explores the sense data and feelings about his perception. He toys with his materials and imaginative responses and transforms them into his imagined conception. When his unique image is given form, a new dance is born.

The choreographer aims to create an illusion so clear that all may comprehend the meaning of the work. He strives to create a unified, well-articulated form that embodies his feelings about some vital experience. He intends that his dance be perceived through the impact of its related forces, of its Gestalt endeavor. The dance as a symbolic form is more than an arbitrary arrangement of movement.

As Langer says,

> The illusion, which constitutes a work of art, is not a mere arrangement of given materials in an aesthetically pleasing pattern; it is what results from the arrangement, and is literally something that the artist makes, not something he finds. It comes with his work and passes away with its destruction. To produce and sustain the essential illusion, set it off clearly from the surrounding world of actuality, and articulate its form to the point

where it coincides unmistakably with the forms of feeling and living, is the artist's task.[1]

BASIC PRINCIPLES

True creative work does not follow any set formula. Composing a dance is not like making a cake; no recipe tells the dancer how to measure and blend the ingredients. The outward organization of the movement must happen because of stirrings within the creator. There are certain basic concepts, however, such as functionality, simplicity, and form, that the mature choreographer knows are significantly related to the making of dances. These concepts are so interwoven into the creative act that it is difficult to isolate and discuss them separately. Yet for understanding we need to examine the meaning and effect of each principle.

Function

The choreographer, in creating a dance, has a motivation that is strong enough and important enough, at least in his opinion, to justify his effort. As a first step in the choreographic process he must clarify the intent of the dance: what is its purpose? Throughout the process he constantly checks his use of material and its manipulation in relation to the function. Does this movement belong? What is its use? Is it indispensable? Is there a more appropriate movement? Does this gesture further the intent? Does this phrase contribute to the overall meaning? The specific intent and nature of each dance determine the directness or indirectness with which it is conveyed to the perceiver. But the choreographer must always strive to transfer an emotional experience to the spectator. This is the basis of the aesthetic experience.

Simplicity

The success of a dance as a work of art is dependent on the economical use of material. Ideally the form should be so organized that nothing can be added and nothing can be taken away. Every movement and quality must belong and contribute to the internal structure. Simplicity does not imply that the dance should be elementary—quite to the contrary. Simplicity in art means that the dance is most effective when the chore-

---

[1] Suzanne K. Langer, *Feeling and Form* (New York: Charles Scribner's Sons, 1953), p. 67.

ographer limits himself to the essentials. He avoids superficial, peripheral, and unrelated ideas. Insofar as possible, he eliminates everything
irrelevant to the central purpose. Every part must contribute to the
whole. In other words he strives for the ". . . wisest ordering of the
means based on insight into the essentials, to which everything else
must be subservient." [2]

As a choreographer matures and gains experience, he is able to perceive, with increased awareness of detail, a greater abundance of sense
data. This mass of stimuli is not overpowering, because the artist's
perception achieves a unity of conception that allows him to assimilate
an abundance of data. The mature choreographer is able to penetrate
the superficialities and eliminate irrelevancies in his search for essentials.
In the same spirit of simplicity, he is willing to work for hours to find
the one true movement.

Form

Form may be described as the organization of forces resulting from
the internal structure of the dance. Form does not refer to the shape of
movements, or to the arrangement of movements, but rather to what
results from the organization. Form, according to Rugg, is ". . . the most
appropriate organization of forces, of relationships felt by the artist,
that he can put down with some objective material." [3] Form gives an
order and wholeness to dance. The internal structure and relationship
of forces within the dance create a sense of aliveness—of something coming into being. Because of these characteristics of wholeness, interre-
latedness, and aliveness, we refer to form in the arts as organic form.

The meaning of organic form and the fact that its power is derived
from the relationship of forces operating within the structure are clarified in Sinnott's statement on the similarities in the organism of living
things and in the organic form in the arts:

> Living things are organisms and organism is, first of all, an organized sys-
> tem of structures and activities. It is not a sprawling mass of semi-inde-
> pendent parts and processes, but is held together under a coordinating
> control. This system is far more significant than materials of which it is com-
> posed—life comes from the relationship among the cells.

Then, relating this process to the arts, he says,

---

[2] Rudolf Arnheim, *Art and Visual Perception* (Berkeley: University of California
Press, 1960), p. 38.

[3] Harold Rugg, *Foundations for American Education* (New York: Harcourt, Brace &
World, Inc., 1947), p. 457.

Just as the organism pulls together random, formless stuff into pattern systems of structure and function of the body, so the unconscious mind seems to select, and arrange and coordinate these ideas and images into a pattern.[4]

So, the life and vitality of dance come from the internal structure and the relationship of forces set in action by the juxtaposition of movement, qualities, and rhythms. Organic form in dance, as in all the arts, is quite different from arbitrary form that is a result of an arrangement of material.

Organic form is the relationship of elements by which a self-determined identity is created with an inherent function emanating from the inter-operations of its constituents, each of which is indispensably related to the whole.[5]

Form is not a thing in itself, but instead it is a symbol that always points to something beyond itself. It is the means of revealing the intent of the dance.

The three basic principles, functionality, simplicity, and form, grow out of the fundamental concept that *form follows function*. This expression simply means that the organization of the dance is appropriate to its purpose. The mature choreographer knows that form will follow function most effectively when the dance is created with great economy or simplicity.

CHARACTERISTICS OF FORM

Although each dance takes the form that it must, certain characteristics are common to all good dances.

Unity

The most essential attribute of a well-formed dance is unity or wholeness. The unified dance gives evidence of developing out of a strong, clear purpose. It unfolds with a directness that seems to penetrate all superficiality and moves toward the heart of the idea. Every part seems to contribute to the whole.

A unified dance is perceived and understood readily because the unity attracts and holds attention. It makes an art object easier to absorb.

---

[4] Edmund W. Sinnott, "The Creativeness of Life," in *Creativity and Its Cultivation,* ed. Harold H. Anderson (New York: Harper & Row, Publishers, 1959), p. 26. © 1959 by Harper & Row, Publishers. Reprinted by permission of the publishers.

[5] John Martin, *Introduction to the Dance* (New York: W. W. Norton & Company, Inc., 1939), p. 59.

A dance made up of many unrelated elements appears chaotic and meaningless. Unity helps the observer grasp central ideas and gives him something to which he can cling and retain in his memory.

From a choreographic standpoint, unity means *selecting, limiting,* and *manipulating.* Since the spectator can attend to only a limited number of movement ideas at one time and cannot grasp a collection of unrelated movements, qualities, and rhythms, the choreographer must select each movement idea with care in terms of its relevance to the function and mood of the work. Then, through a sensitive manipulation of essential material, he must develop the dance and its inherent "holding together" power. Unity, however, is more than mechanical. Real unity in the aesthetic object emerges as the feeling response and inner vision are given visible form.

Variety

Within the unified dance there must be variety. The dynamic tension growing out of the organization of forces gives dance vitality. Contrasts in tension or forces heighten the perception of the pattern of forces and thus contribute to the expressiveness of the dance.

However, the opposing and interacting forces must be kept in a controlled relationship. Unless the forces are held in appropriate balance, the function of the dance can be distorted or destroyed. Although the choreographer should provide enough change or novelty to maintain interest, he should not sacrifice unity. Never should there be variety for variety's sake; variety should be developed within the unified framework. Usually the natural expansion and development of the basic dance idea produces a diversification of material and contrast in quality, rhythm, and spatial aspects that provide variety. Variety achieved in this way maintains its integrity. In significant choreography, attention is focused on the whole, and the parts assume their appropriate place.

Continuity

A dance should be perceived as a continuing experience. It should convey the feeling that it is developing and going somewhere. In some respects a dance is like a story because there is a gradual but steady unfolding of the inner vision of the creator. The observer senses progress toward some undisclosed end. The developing action sets up a state of expectancy and a promise of fulfillment. A dance should be experienced as a happening. The continuity of the dance holds the attention of the observer as well as sustains the vitality and intensity of the experience.

A dance with continuity maintains an orderly flow of its elements and gradually reveals its inherent meaning.

Repetition, important in all of the arts, seems especially important in dance. This is so because a dance, which uses human movement as material, has a relatively short life. It exists only during the performance. Because of the tentative nature of movement, repetition is used in dance not only as a means of conveying the idea, but also as a method of ensuring the observer the opportunity to take in and absorb the movement. Consider the difference in viewing a painting and a dance. When one views a painting, he may study the work or glance back and recheck certain aspects of it; but not so in the dance. The movement exists momentarily and then is gone. Hence the choreographer uses repetition of movement and recurring movement ideas as means of revealing the intent of the dance.

The continuity of the dance also depends on sequence and progression. As movement material is manipulated in relation to its function, it assumes a sequence of action. These sequences must be organized in such a way that they provide for progression within the overall structure of the dance. Within the progression should be a preparation for each new sequence that should be indicated in advance and grow out of the preceding sequence. The spectator must be carried along and the illusion sustained.

The various phrases or sections of the dance are held together by carefully structured transitions. Each transition acts as a bridge that binds together the parts and sustains the continuity of the dance. The transition must grow out of one movement idea and lead to the next. The exact way in which the parts of a dance are related must be determined by the work itself.

Climax

Movement sequences must build to a climax. Within the structure of the dance there is a beginning, development, and resolution. The climax is sensed as the high point within the development. This is the moment of full import, the turning point that leads to the resolution. The dance starts, goes somewhere, and arrives. The climax gives a sense of arrival and completeness.

Dominant points resulting from intensified action are used throughout the dance to differentiate and emphasize the important parts. But the dominant points must be limited to the essentials and placed in the appropriate sequential relationship in order to control the tension aspects of the dance and build effectively to its climax.

Repetition and grouping of movements can be used as means of heightening tension. Also, the organization of forces created by manipulation of the quality of rhythmic and spatial relationships contributes significantly to the kinesthetic aspects of the dance. The powerful climax, however, is not achieved through intellectual planning; instead, like all other significant elements of the dance, it must evolve organically. When the heightening of tension is motivated by an internal ordering, the climax will easily evolve.

Harmonious and dynamic wholes

The choreographer strives to create a dance that is sensed as a harmonious and dynamic whole. It must have a play of contrasting and interacting forces that gives the work vitality, but this action must take place within a unified structure. All its parts must be rhythmically related and held in balance. The movement idea must be organized so that there is a continuity that builds steadily to a climax and fulfillment of purpose. These qualities must be inherent in the dance if it is to be identified as a work of art possessing organic form. This harmonious and dynamic entity called dance is the result of the creator's effort to give outward form to inner responses and images. The form is the creator's means of making his unique statement.

Ben Shahn summed up the purpose of form and its achievement when he said,

> Forms in art arise from the impact of idea upon material, or the impinging of mind upon material. They stem out of the human wish to formulate ideas, to recreate them into entities, so that meanings will not depart fitfully as they do from the mind, so that thinking and belief and attitudes may endure as actual things. . . .
>
> I do not at all hold that the mere presence of content, of subject matter, the intention to say something, will magically guarantee the emergence of such content into successful form. Not at all . . . for form is not just the intention of content, it is the embodiment of content. Form is based, first, upon a supposition, a theme. Form is, second, a marshalling of materials, the inert matter in which the theme is to be cast. Form is, third, a setting of boundaries, of limits, the whole extent of idea, but no more, an outer shape of idea. Form is, next, the relating of inner shapes to the outer limits, the initial establishing of harmonies. Form is, further, the abolishing of excessive content, of content that falls outside the true limits of the theme. It is the abolishing of excessive materials, whatever material is extraneous to inner harmony, to the order of the shapes now established. Form is thus a discipline, an ordering, according to the needs of content.[6]

---

[6] Ben Shahn, *The Shape of Content* (Cambridge, Mass.: Harvard University Press, 1960), p. 80.

A GESTALT ENDEAVOR

Creating a dance, an organic form, is a Gestalt endeavor. The dancer can never work on isolated aspects of the creative act or its product. Whenever he creates, at any level, he is involved in the total act. He may handle some aspects of the experience in a naïve way, but all the elements are there, at least to some degree.

For example, consider the three basic principles of function, simplicity, and form. A newly created work may appear rather unsophisticated in regard to one or all of these principles, and yet each is inherent in the dance. It would be quite possible to evaluate the product—even the beginning dance study—from the standpoint of fulfillment of purpose, economical use of material, and achievement of unity and wholeness. This is not to say that such an evaluation is always desirable with beginning work, but rather to point out that when the dancer creates, he is inevitably experiencing on all three fronts. He approaches the work as a whole and experiences it as a whole regardless of his stage of development.

The Gestalt idea has implications for the learning experience. The first, of course, is that the learner should be encouraged to think of his creative work in terms of wholes. He should try to make a dance that has a beginning, middle, and end. His work should have a purpose, and his material should be organized or formed.

Second, the various and successive experiences in choreography should provide the opportunity for differentiation of the elements, concepts, and principles of composition. This means that the learner needs to focus attention on various detailed aspects of form and study in order to fully understand composition. Through such a process of differentiation and study, the learner gains greater insight and competence.

The third implication has to do with relationships. The principles, concepts, and elements lifted out for concentrated attention and study must be seen in relationship to each other, and each element must be understood as an integral part of the total form. For example, the use of variety or contrast should be studied in the context of the whole dance, never as an isolated entity. Likewise, simplicity, the use of essential materials, should be emphasized in relation to the purpose of the dance.

DEVELOPMENTAL STAGES

It takes time for the dancer to progress to the point at which he can create significant works. The creative development of the young choreographer takes place gradually. He must have the opportunity and the time to grow in breadth and depth of understanding and to progress through various stages of development.

The artistic development of the individual cannot be forced but must be nourished and allowed to unfold. Each individual and unique pattern of growth will take shape in a different way and at a different rate. This means that individuals in a composition class will respond to the same learning experience in various ways. What each person assimilates and takes away from the experience will be in accordance with his motivation, development, and current needs.

The beginner starts his study of composition with his own concept of dance. This concept is the result of his past experience and his ideas of what dance is supposed to be. To some detached students dance is a series of steps strung together. Other students may think of dance as an intensely emotional experience, a time when the dancer releases highly emotional and personal feelings. The teacher's task is to help students discover a true concept of dance.

In learning to create dances as art, each individual usually passes through several stages of development before he acquires a functional concept of organic form. These stages cannot be completely separated, nor can they be neatly categorized. Perhaps they should be thought of as clues to the emergent and developmental nature of creative growth. The following characteristics are typical of progressive stages of development.

Spontaneity

Early creative work in dance tends to be a spontaneous documentation of self. Works are motivated by feeling and sometimes take shape in an explosive or spectacular manner. The creator makes an independent statement through a free unfolding structure or form.

Organization

As the dancer gains increased understanding of the need to select and limit dance material and to make it serve his purpose, his emphasis shifts toward organization. He is aware of movement ideas or the parts of his dance. He uses more repetition, and the dance has some feeling of wholeness. There is a beginning, middle, and end. But in spite of the greater understanding of differentiation and organization of material, the parts of the dance tend to remain constant and appear as separate entities. The dance is organized, but not unified.

Unity

With even greater aesthetic awareness and self-identification with the creative act, the choreographer is able to control his material so that the dance achieves organic wholeness. It has variety in the movement of ideas, and there are changes in the quality, rhythm, and spatial organization. No longer does the movement always assume the same dimension, rhythmic structure, tempo, or quality. There is a deviation from the usual or standard. The dance is more fully developed and achieves a sense of unity and wholeness.

At this stage of development the individual is not always secure with his new insight and skill and, as a result, the quality of his work fluctuates. He may create a dance that in most respects is quite successful. It is motivated, makes imaginative use of movement, and, in general, is well formed—but in the next dance he may regress. One section may seem unrelated to the motivation. It may appear that an arrangement of movement was added because the student's imaginative power ran out, and he, either consciously or unconsciously, added a section. Usually this is a temporary stage, and soon he learns to limit his material to that which is organically related.

Unique expression

Finally the choreographer is able to create a dance at a new level of organization and communication. The work is internally structured and sensitively integrated. It has form. Movement ideas are abstracted and manipulated in such a way that a sensitive synthesis results. The dance now becomes more than an organization, it is an organic form. Although the spontaneity of the early stages of creativity is still an essential ingredient, to it have been added organization and unity. The sophisticated synthesis of movement material is the result of deep self-involvement, clarification of feeling responses, and controlled organization of material. Dance, at this level, is a symbolic form. It is an objectification of human feeling.

CHOREOGRAPHIC EXPERIENCES

The primary task of the teacher is to facilitate the learning experience that motivates and guides the student through the various stages of development. The knowledge and artistic accomplishments of the teacher cannot be handed over to the young choreographer. Only as ideas and principles are experienced by the individual and made a part of his response will they influence his creative work. Hearing and seeing are not enough—the new ideas must become a part of his system. How many times has the dedicated teacher heard a student exclaim, "Oh, now I see! That is what you meant last week." A week later the idea has begun to make sense to the student. Not until it becomes a part of him does it take on real meaning.

The teacher of composition is confronted with several basic questions. What experiences are most effective in stimulating and nourishing the student's creative development? How can he be encouraged to maintain spontaneity needed in art and, at the same time, become more mature in his approach to choreography? How can he best learn how to handle his material objectively and yet not sacrifice the essential emotional base of his art? These crucial questions have no definite answers. Until we have a fuller understanding of human behavior and the development of creativity we need to continue experimenting and using our best ideas.

The early creative work of beginners takes shape as little studies or études. These first projects are concerned with imaginative responses, aesthetic awareness, and organization. Usually they grow out of or are related to movement study. Creative projects at this level encourage the individual to be imaginative and to make something of his own. They are the means through which he gains understanding and skills needed for later work. Many examples of these early projects were suggested in the chapters on creativity and aesthetic awareness.

As the choreographer gains confidence and competence he is ready to concentrate on other aspects of the composition, particularly on meaning and form. No longer is it enough to make a dance; the creative work must convey meaning. The movement must be organized and given form so that it will serve the function of the dance. At this stage of development the student needs an understanding of abstraction as it relates to the creative act. Abstracting is not a new experience to the student, because he has used it throughout previous creative experiences. However, in early projects, action was probably on a spontaneous and unconscious level, and the word "abstraction" may never have been mentioned. For example, when the student used sounds, textures, and imagery as motivation for studies, he was abstracting. He was assessing something from sense data and using movement to convey his responses. But now he must go beyond the spontaneous response. He must understand abstraction and be able to use it knowingly and skillfully.

The choreographer must understand the difference between making a comment *about* an experience and *acting out* an event. Dance as art expresses *ideas about* feelings, not actual feelings. It is a *presentation,* not a representation. The dance presents the inner vision or image of the creator. It acts as a symbol or bearer of an idea.

In making the symbol, the choreographer, in response to some motivation, takes in and absorbs sense data. He may perceive quality, line, and rhythm. These percepts that result from the sense data can be lifted from the specific motivation and then can be recombined in many ways. The manner in which the creator chooses to combine them is determined by the image that has evolved as a result of the original motivation. In this process the choreographer abstracts the essence of the particular situation. He tries to see and feel in depth. He strives to strip away the periphery and get at the core of experience. He abstracts that which he senses as the significant elements of the experience. These abstracted elements are then used as dance material.

The choreographer as artist must understand abstraction as an aspect of the creative act. Through varied experiences in composition he must learn: (1) to lift the abstracted qualities, lines, rhythms from the source of motivation; (2) to remove the abstracted qualities from their everyday settings, transform them to create an illusion, and free them so that they can be manipulated and recombined in the service of the creator's image; and (3) to project this image into a form that is so articulated that the intent of the dance is made clearly apparent. The dance then becomes a presentation of the inner vision, the imagined conception. The original responses and abstracted elements have been transformed into a symbol that is expressive of human feelings.

The phase of choreographic study that concentrates on abstractions may be approached in many ways, several of which are suggested in the following paragraphs.

Animal or bird study

Have students select some living creature that has interesting characteristics and movement qualities, such as the chipmunk, deer, quail, or hummingbird. Tell them to study the particular creature selected and recall their impressions and feeling responses.

In connection with the hummingbird one might think of hovering and vibrating action and quick darting and changing of direction. Suppose these are selected as the significant characteristics or the essence of "hummingbirdness." These sense data then become the inspiration for movement. Improvisation may be used to discover fresh, imaginative movement ideas that flow from this source of motivation. Finally, certain dramatic material is established. The movement ideas are developed, and a dance takes form. The intent of such a dance is to capture the feeling of hummingbirdness in an aesthetically satisfying form. The dancer does not represent or attempt to *be* the bird, but rather presents a comment *about* hummingbirdness. This type of problem tends to stimulate the student to react with spontaneity and imaginative movement ideas.

Nature study

Have students select as the source of inspiration some aspect of nature such as a leafy tree branch, a rock, or the tide. Whatever the source of motivation, they should study it carefully and try to really see it. They should feel into the object and then select the significant skeletal aspects that they wish to incorporate into the dance. Have them explore the movement possibilities before they select and develop the dance.

This type of study, in addition to heightening sensitivity and aesthetic awareness of one's environment, is a means of learning to select and limit material and then to manipulate selected movement ideas. The function of a dance motivated by some aspect of nature may be to capture specific qualities and create a mood. The successful dance of this type is perceived as a play of forces in an aesthetically satisfying form.

Life situation

Have students select some situation or event that stimulates definite feeling response as a motivation for a dance. Examples are "indecision," "a bargain sale," or "a tragedy." They should study the situation from many angles and in different settings and think of themselves and others in this situation. They should abstract certain elements, rhythms, and qualities. For instance, certain gestures of everyday life may be used as dance material, although if specific gesures are used, they must be abstracted and transformed into dance movement rather than performed as pantomime.

This type of problem forces the choreographer to abstract as he creates. To avoid pantomime he must abstract the essence and then create movement that captures it. Movement ideas are then manipulated and organized into a form. The dance, as has been stated before, is not a representation of some specific situation. The movement material must be changed from the original source of motivation and used to build the dance in the creator's image.

Words

Words such as "burdened," "flight," "indecision," "loneliness," and "waiting" stimulate vivid imagery. Since they are related to life situations, they can be used as a good source of inspiration. Consider the word "waiting." Where does one experience waiting? We might think of people waiting for the bus or plane. How do people wait? What have you observed in waiting situations? Do people behave differently? How do the qualities and rhythms in spatial aspects of behavior differ? From this type of exploration the dancer creates certain movement ideas that he uses as the basis of the dance. His finished dance does not represent a specific person waiting. Instead he would try to make a dance about waiting that would incorporate the feeling of "waitingness," and he would try to present his comment about this feeling. The observer's understanding of the dance would result from his own waiting experiences.

Music forms

The student should have occasional experiences working with composed music in order to learn to use music as a source of motivation and to choreograph in relation to the music. This kind of experience should come after he has learned to make dances that express his own ideas and feelings. If he works with composed music too soon, he is tempted to lean on the music to the extent of interpreting it rather than working with it. Music selected for choreography assignments should be suitable for dance and appropriate for the student's level of competence.

To work successfully with composed music, the choreographer must understand its structure and identify its dynamic line and climax. He must become familiar with the rhythmic structure and the dominant points, as well as the quality and mood of the music. With this kind of information about the music, he then proceeds to explore movement ideas and choreograph.

Information about the music serves as background or base but not as the guiding inspiration. The dance must develop as an entity in its own right, but at the same time the choreographer must work with an awareness of the musical structure of the dance. This does not mean that the dance should parallel the music. In fact, the product will probably be most effective if the dance is not parallel. However, the structure of the dance and the structure of the music must work together and compliment each other. The finished product should be sensed as a harmonious whole.

Motivation of student's choice

Since the real purpose of creative experiences in composition is to help the individual learn how to use movement as a means of expression, the classwork should not be so rigidly structured that the student never has a chance to select his own motivation. It is true that the structured problems give the student needed security and serve as a medium through which he gains understanding of design and form. Although the carefully designed problems are the steppingstones that guide the learner through the various developmental stages, it is equally important that each individual have occasional opportunities to penetrate his inner depth and feeling responses for a motivation that seems significant to him. He needs the chance to make a creative statement that is his own in every respect. This is the whole point of the creative development.

SUMMARY

Form is the embodiment of content. It is the means used by the creator to reveal his ideas and feelings. Organic form is sensed as something that is growing or coming into being. Dance as an organic form acts as a symbol of human feelings that evokes aesthetic response in the spectator. In order to achieve a mature work of art the choreographer must have a functional understanding of the basic principles of functionality, simplicity, and form. He must strive to control his aesthetic material so that the finished product has unity, variety, continuity, climax, balance, and harmony.

The achievement of competence as a mature artist takes time. Through his many creative experiences the choreographer must be encouraged and allowed to differentiate and clarify his understandings of composition as well as to heighten his aesthetic awareness and sensitivity.

At every step along the way, the creative experience is a Gestalt endeavor. It is developmental in nature, and each individual must have the opportunity and time to work his way through the various stages of development. Carefully selected and guided creative problems can facilitate the learning and aid the inexperienced choreographer in progressing from the spontaneous, naïve stage to the more sophisticated level of creative work.

Students participating in the workshop led by Alwin Nikolais, 1982. Photograph by Spencer Snyder.

six

Evaluating
the dance composition

Evaluation, an integral part of the choreographic experience, plays a significant role in the creative development of the individual. Controversy is not so much about the *value* of evaluation but about the *process* of evaluation. How to evaluate effectively, when to evaluate, and to what extent—these are the provocative questions that disturb the thoughtful teacher. As we discuss evaluation, let us first look at it as an aspect of the creative act and then explore some of its implications for the learning experience.

Evaluation or criticism of dance involves making an aesthetic judgment that grows out of the observer's perception of the created work. First impressions are usually related to the meaningfulness of the dance and the aesthetic pleasure derived from the experience. As soon as the evaluator, either as spectator, critic, or teacher pursues the experience beyond the first responses, he begins to analyze the work. Through the processes of analysis and synthesis, he clarifies the basis for his impression. These processes then become ones of making aesthetic judgment.

Judging the dance as a work of art is a much more difficult task than evaluating a product that has physical characteristics measurable by some specific standard or rule. For example, the significance of a dance cannot be determined by measuring its length, counting its parts, or weighing its contents. There are no set standards that can be laid against a work of art and used as measurement.

If dances cannot be measured by definite standards, what then is the basis for making aesthetic judgment? Perhaps the first requisite is that the work should be viewed and judged as a totality. A dance communicates through its Gestalt nature and should be evaluated on that basis. Criticism should be made in terms of the specific dance observed. The evaluator of art should not be concerned with judging one work in relation to another. He should be concerned with the qualitative aspects of the single dance. Each work must be analyzed in terms of its own intrinsic nature. The critic is primarily concerned with the full integration of aesthetic material and the unification and resultant communicative power of each dance. Criteria for judging spring from these considerations.

In order for the evaluator to have a genuine response to the dance, he must know something of the context of the work and take time to apprehend the dance as an experience. Knowing something of the background of the dance aids the perceiver in giving himself to the experience and in recreating what has been created. Only in this way can he make a true aesthetic judgment about the unity and communicative potential of the dance. As Pepper states,

> Everyone is expected to be active in his relations with a work of art. For how else can one sense the tensions, and connections, demands, fulfillments, satisfactions and consummation in an organic integration of aesthetic materials, unless one actively enters into them and feels with them as the artist did? [1]

But even when the viewer gives himself to the work, his response and aesthetic judgment will be made with reference to his individual background and experience. As Dewey points out, it cannot be otherwise.

> The material out of which judgment grows is the work, the object, but it is this object as it enters into the experience of the critic by interaction with his own sensitivity and his knowledge and funded store from past experiences. As to their content, therefore, judgments will vary with the concrete material that evokes them and that must sustain them if criticism is pertinent and valid. [2]

Along with the consideration of criticism, it is well to remember that, although all people who view a dance will make some kind of an aesthetic judgment, the nature of their evaluations will vary according to the purpose of the observer. For example, the spectator in the average

---

[1] Stephen C. Pepper, "Organistic Criticism," *A Modern Book of Esthetics*, ed. Melvin Rader (New York: Holt, Rinehart & Winston, Inc., 1960), p. 475.

[2] John Dewey, *Art as Experience* (New York: Capricorn Books, 1934), p. 309.

audience makes aesthetic judgments about the dance in terms of communication and the aesthetic pleasure afforded by the work. The dance critic, on the other hand, has a purpose that extends beyond his personal satisfaction. He judges the work in terms of the significance and value of the dance. The teacher is in quite a different category. His primary purpose is not to judge the greatness of the work, although he is quite aware of its significance, but instead to evaluate the dance in relation to the individual's creative growth. Finally, we must consider the creator as evaluator of his own work. Although we frequently associate evaluation with someone other than the creator, it would be inaccurate and unfortunate indeed to think of criticism as a function limited to an outside source.

One category of evaluation, then, has to do with aesthetic judgment of the dance as an art object, and the other with judgment of the work as it reflects the progress of the creator. In other words, spectator and critic make judgments in terms of aesthetic satisfaction and significance of the work, whereas the creator and teacher of dance judge in terms of bringing the object into being and in terms of the creative growth of the individual. This latter category of evaluation is our major concern in this chapter, since we are particularly interested in the methods of evaluation and conditions that foster creative growth.

CREATOR AS CRITIC

Within the creative act there are reflective moments—a time for conscious or unconscious contemplation about the integration of aesthetic material and the forming of the dance. Throughout the process, the choreographer's aesthetic judgment plays an important role in the ordering of the dance material and the creating of an expressive, symbolic form. This judging, or critical aspect of the creative act, is not a specific stage of the process, but instead, a thread interwoven throughout the experience. The creator's aesthetic sensitivity functions somewhat like a silent partner. It is always present, ready to rush in and assist, or to work silently in the background, or to guide the quiet evaluation that follows the period of "frenzied composing."

Aaron Copland, writing about criticism in relation to music, says that the creative mind must be a critical mind. The composer needs to have critical awareness and to make aesthetic judgment at the moment of creation.

> Composers, especially young composers, are not always clear as to the role criticism plays at the instant of creation. They don't seem to be fully aware

that each time one note is followed by another note, or one chord by another chord, a decision has been made. . . . They are partially aware but not fully aware, and not sufficiently cognizant of those factors which have a controlling influence on the success or failure of the composition as a whole. A full and equal appraisal of every smallest contributing factor with an understanding of the controlling and most essential element in the piece, without allowing this to cramp one's freedom of creative inventiveness—being, as it were, inside and outside the work at the same time; that is how I envisage the "awareness of one's awareness." [3]

The creator's ability to make aesthetic judgments about his work depends in large measure on his own level of aesthetic sensitivity. Since his critical judgment can be no better than his aesthetic awareness, aesthetic growth contributes to critical awareness. So again we are concerned with factors that affect aesthetic growth, critical awareness, and, indirectly, the creative output of the individual.

Rogers and other distinguished authorities in the field of behavior and creativity believe the individual's growth in aesthetic awareness, plastic perception, and creative output is dependent on an inner condition that they call "openness." For the individual to move ahead and develop creatively, he must be able to take in and absorb a flow of new ideas and sensations. Rogers states that the creative output of the individual is directly related.

> To the degree the individual is open to all aspects of his experience, and has available to his awareness all the varied sensings and perceivings which are going on within his organism, then the novel products of his interaction with his environment will tend to be constructive both for himself and others. [4]

This inner condition of openness has a definite relationship to evaluation of the work as well as to the making of the dance. First of all, openness makes it possible for the creator to grow in sensitivity and aesthetic awareness. We know that critical awareness and sophisticated judgment depend on aesthetic growth. So, the conditions that foster aesthetic growth will, in turn, affect the quality of evaluation. Then in quite a different view, openness gives the creator the freedom needed to look at his work honestly and objectively. It allows him to examine the dance on its own terms without any need to be defensive or protective about the product.

---

[3] Aaron Copland, *Music and Imagination* (Cambridge, Mass.: Harvard University Press, 1952), pp. 55-56.

[4] Carl R. Rogers, "Toward a Theory of Creativity," in *Creativity and Its Cultivation,* ed. Harold H. Anderson (New York: Harper & Row, Publishers, 1959), p. 74. © 1959 by Harper & Row, Publishers. Reprinted by permission of the publishers.

According to Rogers, openness to experience means

> . . . the opposite of psychological defensiveness, when to protect the organiza-
> tion of self, certain experiences are prevented from coming into awareness,
> except in distorted fashion. In a person who is open to experience, each
> stimulus is freely relayed through the nervous system, without being dis-
> torted by any process of defensiveness.[5]

This means that instead of responding to the usual categories, the individual is alive to any experiences that fall outside the usual category.
Rogers says that "openness" means

> . . . lack of rigidity and permeability of boundaries in concepts, beliefs, per-
> ception and hypothesis. It means the tolerance of ambiguity when ambiguity
> exists. It means the ability to receive much conflicting information without
> forcing closure upon the situation.[6]

This internal kind of evaluation that springs from the creator's
ability to make aesthetic judgments freely and knowingly would seem
to have far greater value for the learner than the criticism that comes
from external sources. As Rogers points out, the most fundamental
condition of creativity is that the source or locus of evaluation judgment
is internal. The value of his product is, for the creative person, established not by the praise or criticism of others, but by himself. Have I
created something satisfying to me? Does it express a part of me—my
feeling or my thoughts, my pain or my ectasy? These are the only questions that really matter to the creative person, or to any person when
he is being creative.

> This does not mean that he is oblivious to, or unwilling to be aware of
> the judgments of others. It is simply that the basis of evaluation lies within
> himself, in his own organismic reaction to and appraisal of his product. If,
> to the person, it has the feel of being *"me* in action," of being an actualiza-
> tion of potentialities in himself which heretofore have not existed and are
> now emerging with existence, then it is satisfying and creative, and no out-
> side evaluation can change that fundamental fact.[7]

Some recognized authorities who are concerned with creative development of the individual would go so far as to say that dances and other
works of art should be judged *only* by the creator. Others believe that
external sources of evaluation can contribute to the creative development
of the individual, providing judgments are made in the right context

---

[5] Rogers, "Toward a Theory of Creativity," in *Creativity and Its Cultivation,* ed.
Anderson, p. 75.

[6] Rogers, "Toward a Theory of Creativity," in *Creativity and Its Cultivation,* ed.
Anderson, p. 75.

[7] Rogers, "Toward a Theory of Creativity," in *Creativity and Its Cultivation,* ed.
Anderson, p. 76.

and used in the appropriate way. Though there may be some difference
in points of view about sources of evaluation, there can be little doubt
about the power and significance of the evaluation made by the creator.

We know that the serious dance student strives to make each new
work a more accurate presentation of his inner vision. He is quite
aware of the parts of his dance that come out as he wants them and of
other parts that are not right—do not capture his image. He is quick
to recognize problem areas and to seek new understandings and skills.

The individual's work gains in quality as his aesthetic awareness and
understanding expand and deepen. He creates, and perceives that which
he creates, in relation to his current level of aesthetic understanding.
How can it be otherwise? Creative growth, reflected in increased ability
to make dances with greater sensitivity and form, is a matter of releasing and unfolding. As Schaeffer-Simmern has so aptly said,

> Creative growth is an "unfolding" from within the individual, and not
> the result of "stuffing in" from the outside.[8]

The unfolding may take place slowly, sporadically, or at an unbe-
lievably fast pace. But regardless of the rate of development, the exciting
thing about creative development is the great inner source of power that
prods the individual on to discover, assimilate, evaluate, and take the
next step. Man's capacity for discovery and self-actualization is a fundamental factor that should be considered in all aspects of dance education
including the evaluation of works created.

The human being's drive for self-actualization is accompanied by
great capacity for self-direction. He is capable of not only self-directing
his composition, but also of self-directing his search for and use of new
aesthetic understanding. How else but through self-direction could he
perceive his work and make aesthetic judgments about it? The environment can facilitate the perception, but the quality of the dance is improved only as something happens within the choreographer.

The facilitating environment surrounding the creator rather than
critical judgments from external sources must be considered. If we believe that the dance student, given a favorable learning environment,
will identify his needs, reach out for new experiences, and develop his
creative output so that it possesses organic form and communicative
power, then it is imperative that the evaluative judgments from external
sources do not block or stifle the creative responses of the learner. If
we accept this idea about the individual's role in evaluation, then we
must think seriously about its implications for the teacher of dance.

---

[8] Henry Schaeffer-Simmern, *The Unfolding of Artistic Activity* (Berkeley: University
of California Press, 1961), p. 198.

TEACHER AS EXTERNAL SOURCE OF EVALUATION

The teacher, concerned with evaluation primarily as a means of furthering the creative growth of the student, makes aesthetic judgments not in terms of the significance of the work, but rather in terms of the individual's progress and current needs.

The teacher must have basic guide lines to help him in the evaluative process. If we accept the ideas that (1) the inner condition of openness, a lack of defensiveness and rigidity, is fundamental to creative activity; (2) the human being has the capacity and desire to make independent judgments and direct the self through progressive experiences; and (3) the artistic activity and creative growth of the individual will take place in accordance with the natural laws of development and the gradual unfolding of the creative activity; then we have established guide lines with which to function. These concepts suggest that the teacher's role in evaluation is one of facilitating a learner and that evaluation means more than judging for judging's sake.

The function of external evaluation should be to help the young choreographer become more adept in perceiving his work in relation to new aesthetic awareness and in making independent and spontaneous critical judgments about his dances. If the teacher, through evaluation, can help the student achieve these results, the student will do the rest —in fact, he must do the rest, because the teacher cannot do it for him. Each individual must create his own dance.

Sometimes, because of the lack of understanding of creative growth or impatience with the time required for the self-directed approach, the teacher may tell the young choreographer what is wrong with his dance and then proceed to fix it. Of course fixing is done in accordance with the teacher's own image and aesthetic judgment. The modifications or corrections are made with the assumption that seeing the revised dance will further the student's understanding. But does it? It is true that students gain new insight from seeing movement manipulated in different ways. However, the context and procedure for experiences in manipulating movement are quite different from the experience of correcting the student's dance.

This correcting procedure raises some troublesome questions. If the dance grows out of the individual and becomes the outer expression of an inner vision, how can the teacher, as an external source, fix it? Another perhaps more important question is, does this type of evaluating experience release or tend to block the openness of the creator and the natural unfolding of his creative ability?

The fallacy in the teacher's fixing the dance would seem to be in the assumption that the individual will improve the quality of his dances after being told how to organize his material. But we know that he doesn't really learn until he perceives and feels new aesthetic integrations within himself. New insights must be experienced and must become a part of him before they can be functionally related to his choreography. Schaeffer-Simmern, who has done considerable research in creative activity in the visual arts states,

> The configurated visual experience through which a work of art has been conceived and brought forth cannot be replaced by conceptual comprehension. There is a great distinction between information about a thing and cognition of a thing: The one can be learned, the other can only be self experienced.[9]

The evaluation must be conducted in such a way that the creator discerns answers for himself. The teacher must be a facilitating rather than a controlling person. This relationship between the teacher and the student will be apparent very quickly to the sensitive observer. The student's behavior during class activity, and especially during the period of showing and evaluating dances, will reveal a great deal about the feeling relationships and way of working. To test this relationship, visit a class and make two simple observations. First, observe the student's behavior as he goes out on the floor to show his dance. Does he approach the situation with uneasiness and with a cautious eye on the teacher, or does he appear rather confident and eager to show his dance to the class? Are the class members highly interested, or do they seem to be waiting their turn?

Second, observe the student's actions at the finish of his dance. Do he and the other students turn to the teacher with an air of expectancy that seems to say, "There it is, how did you like it? What criticism do you have?" Or does he rejoin the group with a sense of pride and readiness to discuss his work? In other words, is the evaluative pattern one that is built around the expectancy of approval or disapproval, praise or condemnation, by the teacher? Is the teacher's approval the anticipated reward for creative work? Or does the student seem to feel an inner satisfaction that results from his independent judgment about the organization and effectiveness of his dance?

When the evaluative procedure is characterized by students listening in submissive fashion to the teacher's judgment as though his ideas

[9] Schaeffer-Simmern, *Artistic Activity*, p. 199.

were infallible, there is immediate danger of thwarting the creative growth of the individual. This type of expectancy tends to cause the student to try to create dances that please the teacher, rather than dances that fulfill the student's own imaginative conception. Such an evaluative process immediately contradicts and stifles the natural internal unfolding of artistic activity.

Pointing out the danger of external evaluation, Zilboorg states that

> . . . the creative person works within himself most of the time. The best creative work is done unconsciously in the "thou shalt not touch me" sphere of man, and if you open it up artificially and expose it to the gaze of men and make it a matter of technique, you will lose the creative man.[10]

Anderson, commenting about "power over" relationship states that

> . . . this power may be real, potential, or symbolic. It may be intentional or unintentional. The net result of power over another is the ultimate achievement of conformity by the individual to the external standards. It denies to the creative person the opportunity and the right to be himself. It is thus a prime source of anxiety in a person and instigator of resistant defenses. It detracts by that much from the "originality of behavior." [11]

When the teachers' role in evaluating is viewed in quite a different way, without any concern for "power over" relationship, then the function and value of the evaluative experience is a different matter. When the primary purpose of the observation is to further the creative growth of the individual, with no attempt to pronounce judgment on the quality of the work, the evaluative experience can have a positive influence on the creative development of the individual. In contrast to the "power over" relationship, the teacher can create an evaluation situation that is a period of mutual participation. Evaluation becomes a time to discuss aesthetic responses in the sense of sharing reactions. Although differences of opinion may be expressed, the creator always has the privilege of making final judgments about his dance.

Anderson says that this type of external evaluation, "without power over" emerges

> . . . through a process of participation, of two-way communication, mutuality, interweaving of desires, goals, purposes through spontaneousness, meaningful change in interacting with others. This type of evaluative situation becomes an extending experience.[12]

[10] Gregory Zilboorg, "The Psychology of the Creative Personality," in *Creativity*, ed. Paul Smith (New York: Hastings House, Publishers, Inc., 1959), p. 31.

[11] Harold H. Anderson, "Creativity in Perspective," in *Creativity and Its Cultivation*, ed. Anderson, p. 263.

[12] Anderson, "Creativity in Perspective," in *Creativity and Its Cultivation*, ed. Anderson, p. 262.

It stimulates the creator to see and feel with expanded sensitivity, which, in turn, provides a feedback for his own critical evaluation. It aids him in becoming more discriminating and in achieving new levels of integration and unity in his dances. It contributes to the building of a new frame of reference that influences his next creative endeavor.

This sharing process is related to, in fact grows out of, the belief that the individual has the power to guide (self-direct) his creative development and that he must be free to do so. In the words of Shaeffer-Simmern, the teacher must believe that

> . . . the incentive for such [creative] growth lies in the creator's innermost compulsion to proceed to a clearer and richer visual cognition by independent visual judgment of his work. Through this process each successive stage of artistic configuration prepares thoroughly the condition for the formation of the next stage.[13]

In dance this compulsion to clarify and extend applies to kinesthetic as well as visual judgment.

TEACHER AS FACILITATOR

Setting the stage

The teacher is the prime influence in the atmosphere and feeling tone that surround the learner. Since the climate influences the student's reaction to each activity, the student's response to the evaluative period is colored by the emotional climate that precedes and follows the showing of dances. Unless there is a consistency in the teacher's attitude and behavior in all activities, students will not feel that it is safe to venture forth with new movement explorations or to comment freely in the discussion periods.

The atmosphere that pervades the evaluative experience should be stimulating and challenging, but above all it must be free. The individual should be encouraged to reach out for new ideas, to be adventuresome, to examine critically his own work, and to set new goals for himself. The environment should cause the creator neither to feel threatened nor to shut out new ideas because he finds it necessary to be defensive about his work. Instead he must feel that his work has worth and that he is respected as a member of a group that is working toward a common goal. Within such a learning situation is an atmosphere of *with*, not *against*. The student feels free and is open to new experiences.

---

13 Schaeffer-Simmern, *Artistic Activity*, p. 198.

From the first class session on, the teacher should strive to establish and maintain a spirit of seeing and sharing. Students should be encouraged to be concerned with the achievement of class members—to see progress made in handling aesthetic materials, attaining personal goals, and creating dances that communicate. Along with recognizing progress, each individual should be encouraged to identify current needs and set new goals.

When the teacher sets the stage for evaluation in this fashion, when there is respect for each individual, and when the emphasis is on seeing, sharing, and new goals, students are free to perceive and grow. Such a setting does not cause the individual to feel that he is in competition with others or that he must create to please the teacher. Instead he is motivated to move ahead within his own creative world.

Guiding the observation

The teacher must provide sensitive and skillful leadership during the evaluation periods in order to make them good learning experiences. Instead of encouraging an overall evaluation, the teacher should focus the observation and discussion on specific aspects of the work that are related to the student's level of creative development. The student's attention is concentrated on a specific area of composition, and the teacher is able to keep the observation related to current needs of the group. In other words, the teacher should sense the needs of the moment and give a particular direction to the problem at hand.

As the student grows creatively and produces more developed dances, the focus and emphasis of evaluation will shift. This development does not follow any set pattern; therefore, there can be no specific guide for evaluation. However, certain generalizations in creative growth provide clues to the various stages and approaches to evaluation.

During early stages of development, a dancer needs encouragement. He must be helped to gain confidence and security so that he is free to search his innermost self and release his imaginative ideas. Therefore, it is very important that discussion of his work be approached very positively and yet be directed so that it contributes to new perceptions appropriate to this stage of learning. A good approach is to focus the discussion around the question, "What did you find especially successful about the dance?" This question implies that there *is* something worthwhile and also encourages students to look for achievement of their classmates rather than failures.

Some teachers will say that this approach is difficult because beginning dancers often do not have anything of worth. Although this may be so if their dances are being judged against criteria of a mature work, as beginning works and in light of individual progress there is always something of worth that can be pointed out. A student will be encouraged when he hears that some aspect of his dance has improved over his last work. Of course these comments must be honest and sincere, because insincere praise is soon recognized and does more harm than good.

How then does learning take place in this early period of identifying successes? As the class discusses the effective aspects of a dance, every student will be relating the discussion to his own dance. In a discussion of the way a student developed his study out of a single movement idea rather than a series of unrelated movement ideas, every student will ask himself how many ideas he used. Or in discussing the interesting rhythmic pattern of a study and while commenting on its variations, students will examine the rhythmic structure of their own dances.

The motivated individual has tremendous power to relate the newly perceived aesthetic elements to his own work. These new insights will influence his next creative endeavor. A positive approach to evaluation helps the individual realize that he is making progress and encourages him to reach out toward new inventiveness. At the same time, the discussion helps other members of the class identify significant aspects of composition. Obviously, this type of evaluative experience requires a sensitive teacher who can provide subtle guidance.

After students have a certain amount of experience with dance and achieve some confidence, they begin to get curious and reach out for new knowledge related to their specific needs. The teacher must be sensitive to their awareness of need and try to focus the observation and discussion so it will contribute to fuller understandings in these areas.

At this stage of development, good questions to ask are: What do you find most satisfying? How was the movement manipulated in order to solve the problem so successfully? This latter question gives the teacher an opportunity to examine in detail the manipulation and development of movement in one or two outstanding examples. This type of experience contributes to new insight about organization.

When the group is ready, ask this question: Is there any one spot in the dance where you would have manipulated the movement differently —where your imaginative response was different? This question is a means of identifying weaknesses, but it should be asked in the spirit of *sharing*, with the idea that different individuals respond differently and that the final decision should be left to the creator. If asked in this atmosphere, it opens the way for a variety of ideas, stimulates students to become more perceptive, and often helps the creator to find a more satisfying solution. I prefer to start this kind of discussion with emphasis on one weakness so that the main focus remains on achievement.

Finally, students arrive at the point where they want their dance to communicate effectively, and therefore they are interested in aspects of composition that will help them choreograph more effectively. They now have something to say, and they want help in stating it. At this stage of development the focus of discussion may be kept more closely related to the problem than in the early experience. Attention should be given to the specific means used to solve the problem. Observation at this point is more specific and precise but is still positive. For example, the following questions might be used to guide the discussion when the problem areas are as follows:

1. Unity. *What means was used to achieve unity?*

2. Rhythmic organization. *How did the movement structure, movement manipulation cause the rhythmic excitement?*

3. Illusion of space. *How was movement used to achieve illusion?*

4. Abstraction. *How was movement used to give feeling of monotony without becoming monotonous movement?*

5. Climax. *Where was the climax? How was it achieved?*

In the last stage of development the choreographer is quite secure and is highly motivated to create dances that communicate. He is eager to share his work with others and get their reaction. He wants to discuss certain aspects of his dance to ascertain its effectiveness. In this spirit he may ask, "Did you feel ——?" or "Would it help to try ——?" Another student may respond, "I liked that part but it was so short. Have you thought about developing that section?"

Evaluation at this stage is characterized by a free interaction among individuals. This kind of evaluation, which is concerned with the refinement of dances, is a mature response that builds logically out of the three previous stages of observation and evaluation.

EVALUATION POINTS THE WAY

Evaluation plays a significant role in giving direction to the experiences needed to further creative development of the individual and the group. The evaluative experience provides several important opportunities for learning.

First, through the discussion the individual identifies his progress, discovers his particular needs, and sets new goals for his next dance. Second, as the successful or effective aspects of dances are discussed, the students gain aesthetic understanding. Each individual examines his own work in relation to his new insight and tries to use the new understanding in his next creative problem. Third, the skillful teacher, alert to the needs of the group, tries to find an example in the current dances that can be used to illustrate a new aspect of refinement in composition that will help students progress to the next stage of development. Thus, through their present work they identify a new focus that can be explored more fully in the next class session.

For example, the teacher knows that the group is ready to work on development of a movement idea. One of the current dances may have achieved a new level of development. So the teacher takes time to explore this development, its effectiveness, and how it differs from previous choreography of that student and the class. Through exploration and discussion the teacher has opened the way for understanding another aspect of composition and has established a focus for the next class problem.

Fourth, at certain stages of development the group becomes aware, rather uncannily, of the next step or of areas in which they need study. This is especially true of a group after it has had some experience in choreographing. The teacher may realize that the class can progress in several different ways with equal effectiveness. Often he does not have to make the choice. Again and again the focus is set clearly and specifically as a result of evaluation of current dances. For example, students may discover that they repeatedly tend to work in the same stage areas and fail to make use of space. Through discussion they may decide that they should work on the use of space, and thus the focus for the next problem has been identified.

It is fascinating to observe how future goals emerge. To take advantage of this natural development, the teacher must be open to the experience and work with a certain degree of flexibility. Of course, it is ideal from the learning standpoint when the focus for the next class does emerge out of the day's session. The new problem is much less meaningful when the teacher announces it at the next session without students seeing any relationship to their previous work.

SUMMARY

Criticism or evaluation of dance is concerned with the integration of aesthetic material and the communicative power of the work. A dance as a work of art may be viewed from various vantage points and for distinctly different purposes. Yet in any evaluation a judgment is made in terms of aesthetic response to the use and integration of material and the ultimate unification of form.

The evaluator may be interested primarily in assessing the significance of the work, in the aesthetic pleasure afforded by the experience, or in the creative growth of the choreographer. In all cases the perceiver should know the context of the dance and take time to apprehend the experience so that he can recreate the work.

Making aesthetic judgments is an integral part of the creative act, and the creator must work at all times with critical awareness. The level or quality of his critical awareness is closely related to his aesthetic sensitivity and insight. To grow, the creator must be open to new experiences and be able to take in new perceptions that heighten his level of aesthetic awareness.

The natural unfolding of the creative potential is significantly related to the individual's degree of openness and his ability to work with critical awareness. Individuals have great capacity for self-direction. For the individual to use his power of self-direction, the environment that surrounds his creative work must be such that it frees, enriches, and stimulates him to use his fullest resources.

The teacher should strive to establish an evaluative situation that is a period of mutual participation and sharing. When these periods of sharing aesthetic judgment are skillfully guided, the experiences become a source of strength. Evaluative experiences should serve as steppingstones to new sensitivity and choreographic insight as well as point the way for the self-directed creative growth of each individual. The teacher's role in the creative situation is one of facilitation with a deep concern for creating an environment that is nourishing and stimulating. The evaluative experience should provide a learning situation that stimulates the individual to discover himself and to release and expand beyond what he believes to be his capacity.

Photograph by William Ericson.

seven

Designing
the dance experience

THE HUMAN ELEMENT

The process of shifting one's orientation from that of student or dancer-choreographer to that of teacher of dance can be perplexing and even frightening. Such a response is not surprising because the individual must make a complete turnabout, which necessitates adjustments and orientation to a new role. Up to this point in life he has concentrated on his own understanding of dance and worked to improve his competence in dancing and creating. This has resulted in deep self-involvement in the creative aspect of dance.

As a teacher, the individual must shift his attention from a personal involvement in dance to the task of helping students relate to dance. In this reversal of roles the focus shifts from the fulfillment of self to the release and fulfillment of others. If the teacher is dedicated to his task, the adjustment can take place easily, and a new kind of self-fulfillment will result from helping others achieve.

During the early stages of becoming a teacher, many questions must be answered. How does one share this vital dance experience with students? How does one present the integrated complex of dance movement, creativity, art principles, expression, and communication? Where does one start with the beginner, what does one teach, and how does one approach the learning experience? How does one help students unleash feelings and imaginative responses and develop creative potential?

The teacher's rich experience has given him an understanding of dance that extends beyond intellectual comprehension. Through experiencing he has gained a feeling and knowing about dance that cannot be translated into words, and he has acquired a kind of preparation for teaching for which there is no substitute. But now he faces the task of finding ways to establish a learning situation that will enable the student to make these same discoveries about dance.

The young teacher soon realizes that the dance experience must be meaningful to the learner if best learning is to take place. This means that the teacher must understand the student as a learner and think of him as the starting point for the dance activity. Who is the student? What are his motivations? What is his capacity for learning? Answers to questions such as these provide the clue for meaningful experiences.

All students do not necessarily have the same motivations. Some may come with a vital interest in dance as a creative art experience, whereas others may be interested because movement is satisfying. Some may value dance because it is a creative activity, and others may value it because it is a pleasant way of acquiring grace, poise, and physical well-being.

Such differences in perception of dance mean that students start the class at very different levels of understanding and goal identification. This fact cannot be brushed aside by the teacher. Instead he must recognize the necessity of understanding the student at his present level of motivation in order to help him move forward. The teacher can do no more than facilitate and stimulate the student, because the actual change in perception and goals results from an unfolding that takes place within the individual.

Along with the awareness of differences in backgrounds and motivations, the teacher must recognize that the student responds to the dance situation as a whole person—as a totality. He comes with certain feelings that may be identified as eagerness, fear, or indifference. Along with his feelings about dance, he has feelings about himself and about his life. His response to the particular learning situation in dance is affected by all of his feelings. When he enters the dance studio, he does so as a whole person. He does not bring any special parts of himself and leave the other parts outside the studio. Neither can his response be a mechanical one that is produced by the teacher's pushing a button. He responds to every situation, including dance, as a total and unique organism constantly striving to maintain a sense of wholeness and a satisfying relationship to its environment.

Because of individual differences the dance student may not always respond in the same way. Some days he may work with real concentration and the creative ideas may flow freely, but on other days he may find that he has difficulty in giving himself to the situation and achieving satisfying results. He cannot shut out all aspects of life other than dance, and sometimes his response to these other aspects interferes with his work in dance. The teacher must then work with the student as a whole person and think of him as a dynamic organism constantly interacting with his total environment of people, things, and situations.

The task, then, of the artist-teacher becomes one of understanding and accepting students with their present motivations and anticipations; helping them satisfy their immediate goals; and at the same time, stimulating them to extend their horizons and discover the fuller meaning of dance, which, in turn, increases motivation and raises personal goals.

Demands such as these suggest that the artist-teacher must possess an excitement and enthusiasm for dance that is contagious; must function as a sensitive, patient, and understanding person; must be creative as a dancer and leader; and above all, must be able to motivate and help students to achieve beyond what they believe to be their potential. The teacher who possesses these characteristics and gives himself to his work will discover that few tasks can be more exciting and rewarding than teaching dance.

This stress on the student as the focus for the dance experience does not imply that the content or subject matter is unimportant. On the contrary, the quality of the dance experience is of utmost significance in stimulating the learner to expand his understanding and skills. The richer the dance experience, the greater the opportunity for individual gains. But rich content is worthless unless it is meaningful to the student. The better the teacher understands the learner and his work, the more successful the teacher will be in providing a stimulating environment that facilitates learning.

BASIC BELIEFS AND PRINCIPLES

The task of helping the dance student unravel the complexities of his art still remains somewhat of a mystery. Surely the wisest approach is based upon beliefs and principles that are related to the concept of wholeness in the day-to-day learning situation.

From the very beginning, the student should experience dance as a creative art. This is important because the learner's overall impression of dance provides the core concept, limited as it may be, from which further refinements and developments emerge. Each new idea and skill should be seen in a meaningful relationship to the existing whole concept of dance.

It is through such a process that the complexities of dance begin to unravel and are understood. For example, movement qualities should be discovered as a means of evoking feeling states; rhythmic factors should be seen in relation to the aesthetic control of material; and so on. The goal is to discover and understand each aspect in its true context.

The individual's total concept and feel of dance is the matrix from which he reaches out and to which he relates new experiences. As each new learning experience is integrated, the matrix expands and his insight and sensitivity for the next encounter are increased. As an illustration of this growth process we might visualize the dancer as a figure surrounded by a circle that represents his dance world. As each new idea, element, and skill is differentiated, related, and finally integrated with other experiences, the circle expands. This is the growth process, and this is why the learner must have a continual flow of experiences that stimulate and challenge him to extend himself and realize his potential for creative work.

Basic beliefs about designing and teaching dance are derived from foundation knowledge in the area of dance, aesthetics, creativity, and the physical and behavioral sciences. From beliefs the teacher establishes principles that may be used as guides in the process of planning and presentation of dance. The following list of principles emerges from the concepts presented in this book:

1. *Establish a positive learning environment.* The climate should be sensed as free and psychologically safe. The environment should stimulate an openness to new experiences and build students' confidence.

2. *Focus on dance as a creative experience.* Concern should be with expression rather than imitation, and the emphasis should be on feeling, imagining, and creativity.

3. *Experience dance as a whole activity.* Conceive of dance as an aesthetic experience concerned with making and perceiving dances.

4. *Clarify and refine the parts in relation to the whole of dance.* Develop technical skill as needed so that movement is studied as a means and not an end. Expand knowledge of form as the student is ready to make functional use of new insight. Keep new understanding and skills in movements and composition developing in a parallel relationship.

5. *Expand the frame of reference for dance.* Provide sequential experiences that build breadth and depth, heighten aesthetic awareness and sensitivity, and increase understandings and skills.

6. *Develop critical awareness and ability to make aesthetic judgments.* Learn to feel deeply and perceive fully.

7. *Keep the individual as the center of concern.* Think of dance as a human activity through which one creates and achieves his potential, but remember that the individual achieves best in a rich and challenging learning situation. Flexibility rather than standardization stimulates creative growth.

8. *Evaluate in terms of individual growth.* Think of evaluation as a significant aspect of learning, a means of assisting the learner to identify where he is in relation to where he wants to go.

PLANNING

The preparation and planning for a learning situation in dance must be both general and specific. Certain general beliefs, principles, and experiences are common to all dance situations. Yet each specific plan must take into account such factors as the purpose of a particular class, the background and needs of the individual, and the length of the course. The specific aspects of planning do not imply that different kinds of dance should be taught in various settings, but rather that the dance experience must be guided in such a way that it is appropriate for a particular situation.

In recent years there has been a tendency on the part of some teachers to distinguish between what they call educational modern dance and professional modern dance. Such a differentation seems unfortunate, because it is not dance that is different, but the specifics of the situation that differ. Even though this terminology has grown out of a real concern for appropriate experiences in each setting, it would be more accurate and desirable to think of dance as an art experience that is basically the same in an academic or a professional setting. The difference lies in the specific goals and the adaptation of the activity that is determined by the uniqueness of each setting.

Obviously much of the teacher's planning for any situation must happen in the day-to-day context of activities. Even so, some general principles related to teaching are applicable for all teachers. For the teacher to be free to deal with the immediate and specific problems of any group, he needs to be well grounded in general planning. The purpose of this section is to discuss some of the basic principles of planning and methods and presentation that are related to good teaching.

Goals give direction

Basic to planning is the understanding of the learning process and effective ways of facilitating change and growth through the dance experience. All teachers will not establish the same goals; nor will the goals be the same in all situations. But in each case the teacher must clarify the desired outcomes for each dance class and thus establish a direction for action and learning. The following list of goals suggests areas that the teacher will want to consider:

GOALS IN TEACHING CREATIVE DANCE

Appreciation.   Understanding of dance as an art. Awareness of the relationship of dance to the other arts.

Aesthetic awareness.   Increased aesthetic sensitivity. Ability to respond with spontaneity and imagination. Skillful use of aesthetic elements of dance—force, rhythm, space.

Movement.   Awareness of movement possibilities and their inherent expressive potential. Effective body instrument and skill in moving. Functional knowledge of movement principles.

Choreography.   Creative use of movement for expressive purposes. Understanding of form. Functional use of composition principles. Understanding of the creative process. Skillful use of dance accompaniment.

Self and others.   Greater understanding and acceptance of self. Ability to work with self-confidence and self-direction. Understanding of others and skill in working with them.

Evaluation.   Critical awareness skillfully related to the choreographic process. Competence in sharing aesthetic judgment with classmates.

Dance performance.   Functional use of theater crafts—costumes, lights, sets. Ability to relate dance to the stage area and to an audience.

Goals such as these will need to be modified and made more specific in terms of the interests and needs of the individuals in each class. Working with such a list will help the teacher clarify his ideas and establish a base from which to proceed.

Unit plan

The organization of dance experiences, or choice of content, is not a simple process. This is so because dance as a creative activity cannot be categorized and outlined in a tidy, sequential fashion. Much of the time the teacher is concentrating on one aspect of dance but also working on other elements at the same time. Because of the concern for both depth and breadth, the teacher draws constantly from several areas of content.

Each class session should have a focus and direction, but aspects of dance other than the main focus may be interwoven. Confusing as this may seem to the inexperienced teacher, the process cannot be otherwise if we believe that dance should be experienced as a creative activity and that learning takes place best when students encounter whole experiences. The young teacher should know that this very element of flexibility and adaptability that is so confusing at first eventually makes the teaching of dance a creative, exciting, and satisfying endeavor.

Even though dance cannot be categorized, there are ways to organize dance experiences so that they do assume some semblance of order and provide clues for an appropriate progression and relationship among various aspects of dance. The so-called unit plan is a means of achieving such an organization of material. In preparing a unit plan, the teacher should think first in terms of *large areas of experiences* that are related to desired outcomes or long-range goals. These groupings might be identified as movement study, developmental considerations, aesthetic elements of dance, and choreographic experiences. After areas of experiences are established, the next task is to select essential experiences to be included in each area and arrange them in sequential order under the various headings. (See Table 1.) Organizing material in this fashion is valuable because through this process the teacher associates experiences with purposes or functions and identifies experiences that are fundamental. This kind of understanding is essential if one is to build a progression that moves from the simple to the complex and from the core of dance to the differentiations and development.

Table 1

SAMPLE VERTICAL UNIT GUIDE

Movement	*Developmental*	*Aesthetic elements*	*Choreography*
Alignment	Flexibility	Force (energy)	Imaginative response
Balance	Spine	Movement	Organization
Shifting line of	Shoulder	quality	Meaning
gravity	Hip	Rhythm	Organic Form
Torso	Ankle	Pulse	
Shoulders, arms,	Strength	Accent	
legs, feet	Back	Meter	
Moving through	Shoulders	Pattern	
space (locomotor)	Arms	Space	
Elevation	Abdomen	Dimension	
Descending	Legs	Direction	
Turning	Feet	Illusion	
	Endurance		

Another method of organization employs a horizontal rather than vertical arrangement of material. The same major headings shown in the previous format would be used, but the horizontal organization would show relationships and include other factors, such as the goals under each heading. Then the goals would be projected horizontally into experiences, methods of presentation, and evaluative procedures. With this plan one would read in horizontal fashion from the goal, to the experience, to method, to evaluation. Goals in the area such as appreciation and working relationships may be included as well as those specifically related to movement content. (See Table 2.)

The unit plan that is organized around the horizontal arrangement of material has the advantage of pointing up relationships and follow-through. But some teachers may find this organization cumbersome and impractical. They may find it more appropriate to include this kind of

Table 2

SAMPLE HORIZONTAL UNIT PLAN

Goal	Experience	Presentation	Evaluation
MOVEMENT			
1. Elevation	Basic jump	Use of imagery: (A) Feel as though you are being lifted by a string that extends from spine through head (B) Pushing away from the floor	Work with a partner. Observe each other in relation to criteria: Alignment Center of gravity Push-off Extension of ankles, feet Landing
AESTHETIC ELEMENT			
1. Quality (force)	Energy applied in different ways: Continuously Explosively Etc. Exploration of quality: Percussion Sustained Vibrating Swinging	Use short ropes Work with a partner sitting on the floor Improvisation cued by the teacher Short original study using two qualities	Observe studies. Did they understand: (A) Control of energy (B) Meaning of quality
(OTHER GOALS . . .)			

detail in the lesson plan. In any case, the teacher should have some experience with this horizontal organization, because it gives a functional understanding of the inherent process of relating experiences to goals and appropriate methods.

The real purpose of the unit plan, regardless of method used, is to bring ideas and materials together into a functional relationship. Through organization of this kind, one avoids the "shotgun" approach to teaching. Of course the teacher must have flexibility that allows him to work in relation to the need of the moment and the feel of the situation. But if knowledge is to be used most effectively and pertinent materials are to be brought to bear in the most fruitful way, there must be some advance preparation and thinking about total plan.

The format for the unit plan is a device and nothing more. Each teacher should select the format that is most useful in his situation. The overall plan should provide a functional means of bringing together goals or the desired outcome, organization of subject matter, sequential arrangement of experiences, related illustrative material, and ideas for presentation and evaluation. This organization becomes a unit plan. The inexperienced teacher would do well to remember that the time spent in this kind of advance thinking will save time in later planning and will insure better teaching.

Calendar plan

To make the best use of alloted time, whether it is short or long, the teacher should have a long-term guide that suggests spacing of activities, emphasis, and relationships. The calendar plan does not mean a series of specific lesson plans. This, of course, would be a waste of time, because one cannot predict detail so far in advance. The long-term plan or calendar plan simply indicates the day or week when various aspects of experience will be introduced. It provides for a flow of activity and avoids the problem of getting ahead of oneself. It establishes relationships and also ensures the achievement of major goals within a stated period of time.

A calendar plan may be laid out by days or weeks depending on the length of the dance term. Since the major experiences listed in the unit plan are spotted in the time schedule (calendar plan), the various phases of activity must be arranged so that they have an appropriate sequential relationship. This establishment of relationship and flow of activity is important.

It is one thing to talk about what should happen in a dance class and quite another to decide just how to bring the various experiences together in logical progression. For example, should concentration be on rhythm for several days, or should other phases of dance develop in a parallel relationship with the study of rhythm? Should elevation be approached through jumps or leaps, and what preparation should precede this work? Which of the aesthetic elements (rhythm, force, space) should be introduced first? What sequence of creative problems should precede concentrated study of form?

Questions such as these illustrate the problems of sequence and synthesis of experiences. The calendar plan is a tool that aids the teacher in thinking through all that should be accomplished and in planning an effective sequential arrangement of experiences. (See Table 3.)

In addition to the general planning that brings together the projected experiences, there must be some specific planning for each class period. The teacher should approach each dance session with a carefully planned overall view of the day, as well as specific detail of the various experiences to be presented. What should be included and in what sequence? How should the experiences be presented and developed?

The dance lesson plan is usually one of three types. The most common type is conceived broadly and includes both technique and creative activity. A second type concentrates on technique, and the third emphasizes composition. The exact nature of each lesson plan is determined by the needs of the specific group and the best use of class time. All good lesson plans, regardless of type, however, will have common characteristics, because the teacher is guided by certain basic principles. The following five principles are perhaps the most fundamental to good teaching:

1. *Every lesson plan should have a focus.* The focus for a class session grows out of the last session and leads to the next. The design of the plan evolves in relation to the focus, which gives direction and continuity to the class experience.

2. *Each lesson should have a sense of wholeness.* It should have a beginning, development, and conclusion. Experiences in the early part of the lesson should lead the way and prepare the student, psychologically and physiologically, for what is to follow.

The opening activity should not be too difficult or complex. It may consist of new experiences or review of previous work. But in any case it should get the student involved quickly with activities that allow him to perform with a feeling of adequacy. These first experiences should help the student "shift gears," detach himself from previous activity, and shift his concentration to dance. The physiological preparation for the dance activity is equally important. Muscles must be activated and

Table 3

SAMPLE CALENDAR PLAN

Weeks	Monday	Tuesday	Wednesday	Thursday	Friday
1	Introduction to unit	Alignment Line of gravity Torso	Use of feet Locomotor (run)	Quality Response to sound stimuli (percussion instruments)	Show creative problem
2			Continue spotting key experiences and points of emphasis		
3			Continue spotting key experiences and points of emphasis		
4			Continue spotting key experiences and points of emphasis		

Note: The calendar plan suggests sequence and relationship of basic experiences. The lesson plan would be designed around the experiences listed in the calendar plan. Modification would be made according to the progress and needs of the group.

warmed up. The instrument must be made ready for new movement explorations.

The middle part of the lesson should include experiences that require greater concentration and discipline. This core of the learning period should foster new understandings and growth. The content may be new material or new developments of previous experiences. Activity should be designed with a clear relationship to the focus of the lesson.

The last part of the lesson should provide activity that brings together the experiences of the day. A final movement experience making use of the work done during the early part of the period might cause all aspects of the day's activity to fall into place and become integrally related. Or the culminating activity might highlight and clarify certain concepts or principles that were explored earlier in the lesson. This culmination might be achieved through a movement phrase or a creative problem. The exact nature of the ending will be influenced by the focus and particular content of the lesson. The concluding activity might consist of vigorous and exciting movements, such as a leap pattern involving soaring in the air, or it might be a sensitive improvisation resulting in movement quality that is quiet and subtle. The nature of the ending will vary, but every class should give the learner a sense of arriving and concluding.

Perhaps a further comment about the teacher's final contact with the students before they leave the studio is appropriate at this point. Some teachers believe that it is desirable to end the class with a short evaluation period. Surely such an experience can be valuable, but it is doubtful that this ending would be appropriate for every dance class. The conclusion should evolve out of the immediate situation so that it is natural and appropriate. Sometimes it may be very profitable for the group to talk freely about the learning experience of the day and to identify the next step. On other days it may be desirable to use the last few minutes for summarizing and drawing generalizations from the experience. At other times the teacher may close the class simply with "Thank you. I'll see you tomorrow."

3. *The design of the lesson plan should provide for a flow of activity.* The relationship of the activities counts a great deal in the overall effect on the learner of the total experience. Designing a lesson is somewhat like choreographing a dance, because the lesson also must have variety in unity. Sameness is deadly. High-level learning is stimulated by contrasts in activity, but the contrasts must be blended together in such a way that they contribute to an overall balance and unity. There is no formula for the right blend, but there are certain factors that should be considered.

For example, as the teacher plans the sequence of class experiences consideration should be given to (a) the complexity and difficulty of activity; (b) the quality—lyrical, strong; (c) the concentration and degree of discipline required; and (d) tempos or speed necessary for effective performance. The sensitive teacher will plan the progression of activity and determine the length and duration of each experience in terms of the human response. In other words, the sequence should aid motivation, concentration, and giving of self to the experience.

4. *The sequence of activity should be planned with consideration of the use of various parts of the body instrument.* It is easy for the teacher and student to get carried away with some aspect of dance and keep the activity concentrated in a certain part of the body, such as the legs or back, for an extended period of time. This may not be a sensible procedure because, after a certain point, fatigue sets in and the learning slows down. When this happens, it is difficult to continue work with full concentration, and the gains made may not be worth the time spent.

Attention span is another factor to be considered. Although attention may dissipate rather quickly with beginners, in the advanced stages of learning the student brings more to the experience and is able to sustain interest over a longer period of time. However, it is desirable in all learning situations to plan the activity so that there is a shifting or alternating use of various body parts, thus minimizing fatigue and sustaining attention.

5. *The working position of the body instrument should be considered in the designing of sequence and flow of experiences.* Activities may be performed in standing, sitting, lying, and traveling positions. Obviously it would be chaotic as well as a waste of time to shift back and forth between these various positions. To avoid chaos, the lesson should be organized so that the transition of working position is smooth and efficient. Some teachers may prefer to start in the sitting position, progress to standing, and then progress to moving across the floor. Others will start in the standing position, progress to the floor, go back to the standing, and then progress to traveling across the floor. There is not one right way, and probably the order will vary on different days. The important thing is to group activities so that the class is not constantly shifting from one position to another.

Every dance class should have a clear focus. Each lesson should have a beginning that prepares for the major work of the day, a development that emphasizes new concepts and skills, and a conclusion that ties together and sets the learning of the day. Factors such as variety, contrast, groupings, pace, continuity, and flow of activity should be considered so that the learning experience is stimulating and meaningful.

SUMMARY

Good teaching requires thoughtful preparation. The first step in designing the dance experience must be the establishment of goals, which, in turn, cause the teacher to take a long look ahead and identify basic experiences needed to achieve the goals.

The teacher must be aware of his students' backgrounds and consider how they will accept each experience. He must be sensitive to their needs and attitudes and consider them when designing the dance experience.

The serious teacher will find it worthwhile to organize dance experiences into a calendar plan. Such a plan will provide a long-range guide for various phases of development and give direction to the day-to-day classes.

The specific lesson plan for each class must be concerned with the development of various areas of the experience and also the needs of the movement readiness of the group. The good teacher knows that it is the day-to-day planning that carries the work forward in an ever spiraling fashion toward achievement.

Photograph by William Ericson.

eight

Presenting and evaluating
the dance experience

As we have seen, thoughtful planning and preparation are essential steps toward presenting the dance experience. However, the best made plans and outlines are of little value if they are not presented in an effective manner. Excellent content can be lost because it did not reach the student. Only if the learner is involved with the experiences presented will he fully absorb the material and alter his behavior.

No doubt the good teacher will have a kind of intuitive awareness to guide him, but girding his native intuition must be a knowledge of various approaches that contribute to successful presentation.

Multisensory approach

Learning depends on perception of sensory data. Experience supported by considerable research indicates that movement skills can be learned more successfully if they are approached through multisensory experiences. Although each learning experience in movement involves more than one type of sensation, the starting point or action cue may be stimulated by one sensation more than others. In dance, the tendency has been to rely heavily on the use of visual sensation supported by verbal cues. This approach results in the demonstration and analysis method. The student sees the demonstration, hears an analysis, and

133

then attempts to imitate the activity. This is a valuable method, and the teacher should be skillful in using it.

It is unwise, however, to use ony one type of sensation as the approach to all learning. We know that individuals respond in different ways. A stimulus that results in a quick percept formation for one individual may not be as effective with others. A varied approach has a greater chance of reaching more students. It is true, also, that an individual's response is usually strengthened when he is stimulated by multisensory experiences. Dance experiences can be approached through sound and kinesthetic sensations as well as visual sensations.

Since the use of these three types of sensation as a means of stimulating learning have been illustrated many times in previous chapters, perhaps the general idea can be summarized in this way: the teacher is concerned with involving the student in the learning experience. He wants to motivate activity that is accompanied by real awareness and is not merely the result of mechanical imitation. The experience must "get inside" the learner. To achieve these ends, the teacher should emphasize the approach that seems most appropriate for each area of experience. Sometimes he will stimulate the learner by means of visual sensations that result from a good demonstration. Sometimes he will emphasize the hearing sensation as in approaching the study of quality through response to various percussion sounds. At other times he will make use of kinesthetic sensations and awareness that are discovered through movement exploration stimulated by imagery.

The effectiveness of any approach depends in part on the way the experience is presented. The inexperienced teacher may have a tendency to talk too much, which will confuse the student rather than clarify the task.

1. *Choose words carefully.* Use words that convey clearly and quickly the real intent. Remember that different words reach different people.

2. *Be concise.* Use as little talk as possible. Students learn through involvement and experience. Besides, unnecessary words are a waste of time.

3. *Pace the activity.* Keep the flow of activity at a stimulating and challenging level. Provide some variety in pace, but avoid extremes—not too fast and not too slow.

4. *Create a mood.* Use the tone of the voice and manner that sets the stage for concentration and deep experiencing.

Organization of activity

The working position of the teacher in the class situation should be considered. A face-to-face contact with the group establishes a good relationship and ensures ease in communication and observation. When demonstrating or moving in this position, the teacher should reverse his action. That is, he should work in opposition to the class so that when the students are asked to move to their left the teacher moves to his right. This results in a mirroring of each other's movement and makes it easier for students to follow direction. If the teacher turns with his back to the group, he must quickly change so that he moves left when he says left. This system of working in opposition is confusing at first, but after a little experience it becomes an automatic response.

When students are asked to perform movements in a lying position, it is usually best for the teacher to stand. It is wasted effort for the teacher and class both to stay on the floor, because neither is in a position to see. If the demonstration method is to be used, it should be done while the students are sitting, so they can see. Then the teacher should direct and observe the action from a standing position. Unless the teacher can see what is happening, he cannot be very helpful in offering suggestions for improving the performance.

During locomotor movement (traveling across the floor), the teacher's best position is in the middle of the area traversed. In this position he can make comments to individuals as they pass. Sometimes it is advantageous to work temporarily at the place where students start moving and then resume position in the center area.

The teacher's position should be functionally related to the accompanist at all times. The musician should be able to observe the teacher's movement and also to be able to hear what is being said. The teacher and musician should establish a working relationship that is comfortable and functional.

During the major portion of the class period, students will probably work in unison. But in some instances it is advantageous to have the students arranged in two or more groups. Group 1 performs a series of jumps followed by Group 2, and they continue alternating. The brief recovery period between performances postpones fatigue and allows the student to continue with full performance for a longer period of time.

Movement patterns requiring traveling or progressing through space demand a different method of handling the group. The method will depend on the teacher's preference and the nature of the activity, but it is well to know several ways of planning this phase of the activity. Several of the most frequently used organizational patterns are described in the following section.

FIG. 1   The class moves informally around the room in a
circular pattern.

The main advantages of this method are that a large group can be handled, everyone is kept active, and individuals feel comfortable because they are absorbed in the group. Disadvantages are that continuous activity may cause fatigue and thus decrease efficiency. Also, sometimes when students perform *en masse,* they waste time because they are not motivated to give their best.

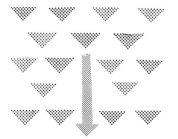

FIG. 2   The class moves as a
group, *en masse,* across the
floor.

This method is especially good for first stages of learning when marking or walking through the activity. The whole class explores together the pattern before performing it fully and moving in sequence. This brief group activity economizes time because it clarifies the activity, straightens out problems, and thus avoids wasteful repetition.

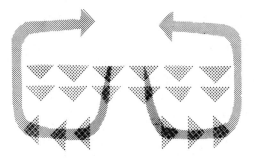

FIG. 3   The first group
moves down the floor, then
divides and walks around the
sides of the room, returning to
the starting position.

Large groups can be handled rather easily with this method. People are kept active and piling-up situations are avoided. The continuous movement may help to hold attention. This method is probably most effective in situations such as a master class where large groups must be handled.

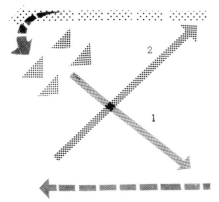

FIG. 4 Small groups move diagonally across the floor (path 1), walk across the end of the room, return on the opposite diagonal (path 2), and walk back to the starting position.

This method, used more frequently than any other and probably to better advantage, makes good use of space by providing a longer path of action. The walk across the end of the room to a new starting point provides a brief rest period and also keeps a large group moving and under control. Perhaps the most important advantages of this method are: (1) students are motivated to give their best and perform more fully when they move across the floor in small groups rather than when they move en masse; and (2) the teacher has an opportunity to observe each individual and make suggestions; hence teaching is better.

FIG. 5 Groups move diagonally across the room in an alternating pattern. Each group starts on a new phrase. For example, the first group comes from corner A on phrase 1, corner B on phrase 2, corner A on phrase 3, corner B on phrase 4, and so on.

This organizational plan requires a high degree of alertness to the starting cue. Its demand for good rhythmic response makes it stimulating and challenging.

The teacher should remember that each of these organizational schemes may be confusing to students when they first experience them.

A great deal of time will be saved by taking a few minutes to explain the system and walk through the pattern.

Preparing for creative projects

The inexperienced student will respond more fully and imaginatively when the creative problem or choreographic assignment is an integral part of the lesson plan. It is usually better to plan the movement experiences so that they lead up to and prepare for that which is to follow, rather than teaching isolated techniques during the first part of the period and then making an abrupt shift to the creative project. This kind of preparation should provide readiness for imaginative experiences and an understanding of the problem.

Suppose that the creative problem is concerned with the use of gesture as dance material. As preparation for this problem the teacher might use guided exploration and improvisation as a means of teaching. Through these experiences and related discussions the student will gain a greater understanding of the artistic process involved and in so doing will build a psychological readiness for the creative work.

As another example, consider a space problem in which the emphasis is on the use of planes. The teacher would likely introduce the concept of planes in the early part of the lesson. These ideas would be explored in relation to the movement study and various techniques. The meaning and use of planes might be clarified through the use of some visual material such as pictures or rope manipulation. The creative problem would be sensed as a natural extension of preparatory experience. The dancer would use his new understanding in his own imaginative way.

The transition from the teacher-directed activity to the individual or group project is a crucial point in the lesson. The established mood and readiness must be sustained, which calls for a skillful transference of leadership from teacher to student. The choreographic assignment must be set in such a way that it has clarity and also stimulates inventive and imaginative responses. This means taking enough time to define the problem and to suggest various possibilities. Illustrative materials such as pictures, objects, and demonstrations may be used to clarify the problem and to stimulate the student's creative response.

Finally, the assignment should be restated or summarized. At this point, the student should begin to respond with his own imaginative ideas and be ready to go to work. If he is hesitant and appears to be perplexed, the teacher probably did not do a good job of preparing and presenting the problem, or the problem was not appropriate for the student's particular level of development. In this connection, it is important to remember that the first creative assignments should be structured so that the student has something to support him. But within the structure should be an opportunity for imaginative and creative response. As the student develops creatively, the problems will shift gradually from the structured to the unstructured.

When should the early creative work of students be shown? This question arises from the teacher's concern about the student's welfare and the best use of the classtime. There should always be some recognition or response to creative work accomplished, although every study need not be performed in front of the class. The teacher must determine the nature of the showing in light of the student's readiness to perform in an imaginative stage setting and the value of showing in relation to cost of time consumed.

Since the very early creative studies are designed primarily to encourage the student to respond imaginatively and to use his ideas, it may not be worthwhile to spend much time in seeing these. Besides, the student is usually hesitant about dancing before the group at this stage of development. The important thing is to recognize that the student has created something of his own.

There are several ways that the early studies can be quickly shared with the class. For example, if the creative problem uses some simple locomotor activity, it may be possible for groups of two or three to progress across the floor in a diagonal path. The students would then show their work by performing in sequential fashion, one group following another, so that there is a continual feeding in of groups. This culmination of the project would be satisfying and would save time. When students perform their work in this sequential fashion, they don't worry about the presentation because they are so absorbed in the total group movement that they don't feel conspicuous. Thus they are comfortable and perform more fully.

In studies that use limited space, the teacher may have one-half or one-third of the class show their work in the area where they have been working. Each study will not be seen fully when several are shown at the same time, but it may be more important to help the student feel comfortable and to save classtime for other activities. With his group approach the teacher can make general comments that highlight some of the interesting results or approaches used in the studies.

As an intermediate stage of presenting works, students may perform in the area where they have been working. While all groups are seated in the work area, the performance progresses quickly around the room from one group to another. In this way each group performs before the rest of the class. This method, which saves time and helps the student feel more at ease, is a good preparation to performing in an imaginary stage area before the class. The teacher should encourage students to observe interesting aspects of the various dances.

As soon as the students are ready, they should begin to present dances in front of the class. One area of the room may be designated as a stage area, and the class may be seated at the opposite end of the room. At this point the presentation is used as a means of encouraging the student to share his work and to learn to observe and make aesthetic judgments. The teacher establishes criteria and guides the evaluative discussion in accordance with pupils' level of development and the needs of the group.

Use of illustrative material

Getting the student to think about and feel the new concept (the movement pattern or the choreographic principles) is probably one of the greatest challenges of teaching. Sometimes this goal is achieved by stimulating the learner to create some kind of an image that causes him to perceive more fully and experience more deeply.

Illustrative materials used wisely can effectively capture interest and stimulate the individual to think and feel. It is a matter of selecting and relating the wealth of useful material that is available. The following list suggests some illustrative materials.

Materials	Dance experiences
Pictures, art objects	Basic art concept
Dance photographs	Movement principles
	Design
	Use of theatercraft
Music composition	Form concept
	Quality, tone color
Dance films	Choreographic concepts
	Movement principles
Objects: driftwood, feather	Textures
String, rope	Planes: vertical, horizontal
Percussion instruments	Rhythmic organization
Human skeleton	Relationship of body parts
	Movement principle
Plumb line	Gravity principle
Elastic band	Tension, release
Bouncing ball	Rebound principle

The effectiveness of audio-visual materials also depends on preparation; taking them to class is not enough. Illustrative materials must be integrally related to the total experience. Timing is important. Material used at the right moment can be highly effective and at the wrong moment, ineffective. Since materials should be introduced without breaking the continuity or mood of the class, they must be organized in the order in which they are to be used, and they should be conveniently located. The teacher leads up to this experience the same as any other movement experience. The transition with the visual material and then back to the aspect of the lesson that follows should be planned carefully. Preparation of illustrative materials requires time, but the results are rewarding.

Related experiences

The content of the dance class can be enriched immeasurably through the use of related experiences. Students should be encouraged to attend concerts, to see art exhibits, to observe selected samples of architecture, and to study the wonders of nature. Whenever possible, these experiences should be related immediately to the dance class. Taking class-time to prepare students for what they are to see or hear and then discussing their observations is often a wise use of time. Since the student of today is confronted with so many opportunities to see and do, he is apt to let valuable experiences pass by unnoted unless events are brought to his attention and made meaningful.

Classwork should be supplemented and supported by reading assignments. Students will want to read dance literature that is appropriate to their particular work. Knowing something about dance personalities, philosophical concepts, historical developments of dance, and principles of choreography will help students discover the real meaning of dance. Their work should not be limited to dancing and talking about dance.

EVALUATION AND GRADING

Evaluation is the process of assessing the individual's progress or growth; that is, seeing his current work in relation to where he was and where he wants to go. Grading is the process of measuring the individual's achievements against established standards. Both processes, evaluation and grading, have a place in the learning experience, but the two should not be confused. Let us examine evaluation as a part of the teaching process.

Through evaluation the student can be helped to see his present level of development in relation to the desired outcomes, to identify specific needs, and to set new goals. Guided evaluation experiences included as an integral part of the dance session should make a significant contribution to the growth of the individual. Both the teacher and student assume responsibility for these sessions.

Some kind of evaluation should be planned for the major areas of learning, which we might identify as (1) movement—use of the body instrument and movement skills; (2) composition—the creative use of movement for expressive purposes; (3) knowledge about dance—functional understanding of words, concepts, principles; and (4) social growth—acceptance of self and good working relationships with others. Different methods of evaluating will be needed, and each category should be approached in an appropriate and meaningful way. Several suggested procedures for each area are discussed in the following section.

Movement evaluation

Students like to be observed and to receive specific suggestions for improving their performance. In a large class it is difficult for the teacher to give a lot of individual evaluation. A good supplement to the teacher's evaluation is partner observation. In this procedure the teacher guides the observation by pointing out certain things to be considered in the performance of a specific movement pattern. Then the student observes his partner and follows up with suggestions. This procedure is not only a method of helping each individual identify his specific problems, but also an excellent means of improving the observer's perceptions. This partner evaluation can be planned in such a way that it consumes very little classtime. For example, following a work session on some particular pattern such as plié, turn, or run, the teacher may take a few minutes for partners to make observations before going on with the lesson.

Working with students in small groups is the next best thing to working individually with each student. Periodic evaluation of this type can be rewarding, although it may only be feasible at strategic points, such as the end of a certain phase of work, midterm, or close of a unit.

For the teacher to be free to work with groups of three or four students at a time, there must be careful organization of the class period. First, students must be grouped so that the teacher can move quickly from one group to another. This may be accomplished by having the teacher stationed at one spot and having the group come and go on call. In some instances it may be better for the teacher to progress around the room from one group to another. Second, activity must be provided for the total group. Students must have something worthwhile to do while they wait their turn for evaluation. Probably the easiest way to balance the time, is to have them work on choreographic assignments but other tasks can be appropriate and valuable, too.

Teacher preparation includes planning the activity to be evaluated and the criteria and procedure for evaluation. If the teacher is going to look at alignment, plié, and jumps, he must first decide what specific points are to be discussed in each movement and how observations are to be recorded and discussed with the student. Observation takes less time when one does not make a record, and in some instances this procedure may serve the purpose. At other times it is important to record the findings so that the record may be used in a later conference, or may be compared with other records to determine progress. Also the inexperienced teacher will find that the act of recording will sharpen the observation.

The teacher may decide to use a very simple evaluation form. For example, it may include the activity to be evaluated and certain items to be observed. In jumps, for example, one might decide to observe alignment, push-off or thrust, and landing. This type of evaluation guide assumes that the teacher knows how to make specific observations, such as action of the feet and ankles.

A more detailed evaluation guide may include fundamental considerations that relate to all movements. Such a form may include such items as control of balance (alignment), control of energy (tension-release), range of movement (joint and spatial), coordination of movement, and rhythmic accuracy. (See Table 4.) The observer would evaluate each movement pattern in relation to these factors. This procedure requires more time but has the advantage of directing attention to fundamental rather than superficial aspects of the movement.

The video camera as an evaluative tool is fast becoming a practical reality. Through the use of this device the dance student can gain a great deal through self-evaluation, which means observing and evaluating himself rather than depending on another person's evaluative comments. The video camera and monitor can be used for observing both locomotor and nonlocomotor movement. In nonlocomotor movement the camera can be focused for a front, side, or back view so that while the individual is looking straight ahead at the monitor, he can see his performance from the front, side, or back.

The teacher can guide the student by pointing out certain things that are observable, such as extension of the foot, alignment, or high shoulders, or by encouraging the student to make his own observations. The latter method is pursued through leading questions, such as "What do you see in the feet?" "In the shoulder area?"

Table 4

SAMPLE EVALUATION GUIDE
FOR THE TECHNICAL ASPECTS OF MOVEMENT

Name: ....

Date: ....

Movement pattern	Control of alignment (balance)	Control of energy (increase-decrease)	Range of movement	Coordination	Rhythmic accuracy
LEAP	Keep the shoulders over the hips Avoid hyperextension in the lower back	Relax the shoulders	Extend the ankles Point the toes		Don't rush; sustain movement in the air
TRIPLET RUN	Shift weight forward over foot	Relax ankles on landing	Lengthen steps		Keep steps even and smooth

(OTHER PATTERNS . . .)

This latter approach tends to make the student really see and understand. He learns to perceive more fully and to relate his performance to movement principles. The fact that the camera can be focused on a specific portion of the body has a real advantage over observation in the mirror. When the student sees only a part, such as the feet and ankles, or feet through knees, he is able to concentrate on a specific concern and is not so apt to be distracted by observation of other parts of the body. Thus his perception of the specific is greater.

The use of the camera need not be limited to assessing movement. It can be a means of learning as well as evaluation. As the student observes himself, he should have the opportunity to make a few tries at adjusting and improving his performance. When the observation and adjusting process is guided by the teacher's comment, a great deal of learning takes place in a few minutes.

Self-observation of locomotor activity is a little more difficult, but camera and observation skills can be acquired quickly. In these activities the camera must follow the dancer, and the dancer must watch the monitor as he moves forward. The camera has a tremendous advantage over the mirror for observation of locomotor activity, because it allows the dancer to look straight ahead at the monitor and at the same time see his movement from the side.

For example, if a student wished to observe his leap, the monitor would be placed at one end of the studio and the camera in the center area so it can follow the dancer and get the side view. The student leaps across the floor facing the monitor. As he looks straight into the monitor he is able to observe a side view of his movement. He can observe the control of torso, alignment, weight distribution, spread of legs, and use of feet. One such observation of self in action is worth several comments from the teacher.

Videotape is fast becoming a practical means of evaluating movement and can be especially useful in observing locomotor activity. It is now possible to record a sequence of movement, push a button and play back the picture so that the student sees his movement, and then push a button that prepares the tape for recording the next student's movement. Through the use of the video camera and videotape the choreographer is able to see his dance and react to his own visual impression. No longer does his aesthetic judgment need to be limited to his kinesthetic response and the comments of others. There is no doubt that the camera, with videotape and the monitor, can be an extremely valuable tool in evalua-tion and learning. What we need now is experience and research that will help reveal the full potential and functional use of video.

The advent of hand-held video cameras and inexpensive portable VCRs (videocassette recorders) has greatly facilitated recording dance movement. The camera need not be stationary. One student can be assigned to be the camera operator while another performs a movement. In this way, the movement can be recorded from a variety of angles as it is executed. Even the less-expensive video cameras usually have a zoom-lens feature, allowing the camera operator to "zoom in" on one portion of the body as it moves. The tape can be saved and replayed many times, which can greatly facilitate study.

Schools with more elaborate television studio facilities can use multiple cameras to record a dance performance. The different shots are then edited onto a master tape that can more accurately reflect the complexity of movement in a piece. Videotaped performances are excellent and inexpensive ways to build an archive of dance material for later teaching, departmental recruitment, and obtaining performing engagements, as well as for preservation. Students can make copies of tapes of their performances for use in professional auditions.

Composition

The evaluation process will vary depending on the purpose of the choreographic assignment and the developmental stage of the dancer. However, the teacher and student should always use some kind of focus or criteria as guides for the evaluation, regardless of the method used. The focus will, and should, vary greatly. Beginning dance studies may be observed and evaluated in relation to a single factor or question, whereas mature dances may be viewed in relation to broad criteria.

One means of establishing the focus for observation is through the use of selected questions, such as, "Does the dance convey the intent of the choreographer?" Or, more specifically, "Is there a contrast in the rhythmic structure?" The teacher may wish to involve the class in identifying the specifics to be considered in evaluation and in this way prepare them for the observation.

Mimeographed forms are sometimes useful as guides for observation of creative work. Such forms are especially useful when students have developed some competence in composition and ability to perceive. (See the sample evaluation forms, Tables 5 and 6.) Table 5 has space for specific criteria. Table 6 is designed on a broader base, which means that the student must draw upon his understanding of each criteria. Evaluative forms such as these give each student a chance to express himself. The written form may encourage the quiet student to become more involved in the evaluative process.

The written form may be related to evaluation by asking students to use their written responses as a basis for the class discussion and then to give the statement to each choreographer or the teacher. The written evaluations will reveal something of the observer's understanding of composition as well as his level of perception.

Knowledge about dance

Knowledge about dance includes primarily functional understanding in the area of movement and composition and in some instances the historical and philosophical aspects, as well as appreciation, of dance. Evaluation of growth in knowledge must be measured by oral or written methods. Whether oral or written, the evaluative schemes should be designed to reveal the student's understandings of concepts or principles

Table 5

SAMPLE EVALUATION FORM (SPECIFIC)

Name:.................................   Problem: Asymmetrical use of movement

Criteria *	Yes	Partially	No
1. Asymmetrical movement	....	....	....
2. Variety	....	....	....
3. Continuity	....	....	....

What aspect of the dance was most satisfying?...

....

....

* Used to focus observation and evaluation on certain criteria that are related to the specific problem.

Table 6

SAMPLE EVALUATION FORM (BROAD BASE)

Dance title:...............................   Performed by:...........................

	Yes	Partially	No
1. Is the intent clear? (function)	....	....	....
2. Is the movement idea developed?	....	....	....
3. Is the development handled with economy? (simplicity)	....	....	....
4. Is the organization effective? (form)	....	....	....
5. Is the dance successful from the standpoint of:			
Unity	....	....	....
Variety	....	....	....
Continuity	....	....	....
Climax	....	....	....

6. What do you find most pleasing or satisfying in the dance?...........................

....

....

that have been studied. Several approaches to this kind of evaluation are suggested in the following section.

Short quizzes or longer examinations may be used. The type of questions, essay or objective, should be determined by content to be evaluated. Another method of assessing understandings might be through matching words or through defining selected words. The dance student must build a rather extensive vocabulary. Usually this knowledge evolves indirectly from the movement experience, but regardless of method of learning, the dancer must have a functional understanding of many words, such as these:

Contrast	Meter
Release	Tempo
Extension	Phrase
Movement quality	Unity
Asymmetrical	Climax
Accent	

A summary statement written by a small group may be a useful means of evaluation. The group may discuss a certain topic related to a reading assignment, movement concepts, or principles of composition. Following the discussion, they write their conclusion. Such a procedure gives the students an opportunity to clarify and integrate their ideas. Material that they develop may be shared with the class in discussion or used in conference with the teacher.

Sometimes functional understandings are best reached through demonstrations. For example, the student may be asked to illustrate selected concepts or principles through performance rather than through oral or written communication. When demonstration is used, the student performs his "movement answers" for the class. Such an evaluative process makes it essential for the dancer to be able not only to verbalize, but also to *apply* basic understandings. The presentation in class affords a good opportunity for clarification and learning on the part of all students. The following topics suggest the content that may be evaluated through demonstration: flexion extension; movement quality; shifting center line of gravity and shifting body weights off center line; symmetry and asymmetry; mixed meter; syncopation; or a phrase.

Personal and Social growth

The significance of dance as one of the arts arises not only from the aesthetic value of great choreographic works, but also from the value of the creative art experience as a medium for self-actualization of the individual. In one sense the personal growth is an indirect development. Dance as a specific area of learning is concerned with understanding and skills in dance, around which class experiences are centered.

The specific objectives of most dance classes should not be stated in terms of social development of the individual. Yet one of the real values of dance in our society is that dance as a creative experience helps man better understand himself and relate himself to his environment. This is one of the reasons that dance has a justifiable place in the academic setting. If one accepts this value, then the teacher of dance should have some concern about what is happening to the individual as a result of the dance experience. It would seem desirable to provide for some kind of evaluation in the area of personal growth.

Of course each teacher must use methods that are appropriate to the situation. Large classes and limited time make it necessary to streamline the evaluative procedures, which at best can be time consuming. Within each class there should be some functional means of keeping contact with individual growth. This may be done through teacher observation, rating scales, student self-evaluation, student diaries, and conferences. Several of these methods are discussed in the following section.

The teacher has an excellent opportunity to observe student behavior in many situations during regular class activity. The student's attitudes, appearance, and response to the activity, as well as his relationship with other students and the teacher, may reveal important clues to personal growth. The skilled observer will be sensitive to behavior that reflects responsibility, contribution to the class, creativeness, leadership, adjustability, concern for others, serious purpose, emotional stability, and response to difficulty. Through observation the teacher becomes familiar with typical behavior and learns to recognize the exceptional. Observation over an extended period of time provides clues to significant changes in behavior patterns.

The unrecorded observation makes the least demand on time and is the method most frequently used. But the recorded observation gives a more accurate picture of trends and behavior. It also ensures that the less noticed students are observed. If there is not time to keep this kind of record on each student, the teacher will find it useful to select certain students for observation and careful evaluation.

The anecdotal records containing descriptions of behavior in different situations, should be specific and should not include the teacher's interpretations. This type of record is worthy of study and practice. There is probably no better way for the teacher to become a sensitive observer than through keeping anecdotal records.

The student should have some opportunity to prepare his own self-evaluation, which can be done in several ways. A carefully designed rating scale may be a useful technique to direct attention to certain aspects of behavior and to help the student determine his progress. To rate himself he must think about his behavior in various situations. A rating scale might be structured in the following manner:

1. I contribute to group projects
always..........usually...........sometimes...........rarely..........never...........

2. I participate in evaluative discussions of dances
always..........usually...........sometimes...........rarely..........never...........

In contrast to the highly structured rating scale, the teacher may wish to use the open-end, free-response written evaluation. This type of evaluation aids students in identifying progress and in establishing a focus for their next period of study. This method requires carefully designed questions that direct the students' attention to specific areas of behavior but at the same time keep the response broad enough so that the students are stimulated to think of various situations and respond freely. Students seem to find this type of evaluation valuable and satisfying. It causes them to withdraw momentarily from the onrush of activity and think about what has taken place; a thoughtful evaluation can be an integrating experience.

Sample

> Write a summary statement of your evaluation of your growth. As you come to the end of this term, it is appropriate that you take stock. Consider your present stage of development and the progress that you have made. Then identify your current needs and goals. Take time to do a thoughtful job. Consider what has happened to you as a result of all your class experiences.

The individual-student conference is probably the most valuable of all the evaluative techniques. At this time the teacher and student discuss the results of observation and related information to compare ideas about the student's progress. This experience can be especially meaningful because it is highly personal. The student knows that the discussion relates to him, and at this point he is no longer one of the crowd but the center of attention. Of course the sensitivity and skill of the teacher are real factors in the effectiveness of the conference, and perhaps of greatest importance is the teacher's sincere interest in the student and his growth.

Many teachers interested in working with students ask, "How does one find time for conferences in the midst of large classes and increasing demands on the teacher's time?" Of course conferences must depend on the opportunities available in each specific situation. But if the teacher is sensitive to the value of his personal contact with students, perhaps some time can be found. Often three or four minutes spent with a student at the close of class can be rewarding. Also, if there is not time for scheduled conferences, perhaps the teacher can be available to those students who need and seek his help.

GRADING THE DANCE ACHIEVEMENT

In many, if not most, school situations grading is used not for appraising the progress or growth of an individual but for judging his achievement. This assessment, given as a letter grade, is made in relation to set criteria or standards of achievement. At a specified time the student's work is measured and graded.

Most dance teachers find grading a frustrating experience, because it seems to deny the philosophy that has guided their teaching throughout the creative learning experience. They have been concerned with student growth and have tried to help each individual progress according to his own developmental needs. They have de-emphasized conformity, competition, and set standards in order to free students to work creatively. Day-to-day evaluations have been concerned with progress and individual needs. Then, at midterm and at the end of the semester, the teacher is faced with the necessity of reporting a specific grade for each student. If these grades are computed in the traditional way, the achievement of a student must be judged by certain criteria.

One may feel that such a procedure contradicts everything we say about evaluating a dance and seems to be in direct violation to all that we believe about ways to further creative growth of the individual. But until a different system of grading prevails, the dance teacher has no choice. Somehow he must incorporate marking in the overall experience and use procedures that seem most sensible.

The teacher not only must clarify his ideas about grading in relation to his larger concept of evaluation, but he must also help students recognize the difference in evaluation of growth and measurement of achievement. The student should be realistic about the meaning of marks and at the same time should understand that his growth is the most important thing. Most students will understand this if teachers are skillful in helping them see marking and growth evaluation in the proper context. At some point the student should be involved in identifying and discussing the criteria for grading. This makes the final reckoning a little easier for the teacher and the student. If criteria and grading are handled wisely, this final letter grade can be a means of helping some students become more realistic about their achievements.

Although teachers have different ideas about grading criteria, the major emphasis should probably be on understanding and skills in the dance area. Such things as attendance and care of costumes, although important, are in a different category. Perhaps the teacher should assume that students will take responsibility for these peripheral obligations, and perhaps laxity in these areas should be reflected in the grade, but not through a complicated point system. Emphasis should be on learning, not on conformity to certain rules.

Since marks are symbols that have certain meanings in academic circles, the dance teacher has little choice but to fit into the scheme.

As long as an "A" means outstanding achievement, we would do well to have "A" represent outstanding achievement in the creative world of dance. Some people suggest that students in the arts should be marked pass or fail, thus avoiding a dilemma; but such a policy would only create another dilemma. If dance and other arts have a justified place in the academic world, then the dance student's achievement should be recognized and receive grade points in the same manner as achievements in other areas of learning.

With the increased emphasis on quality in all phases of education, the dance teacher must lift his sights and constantly enrich and improve the quality of the dance experience. This goal can be attained without violating the true concern for creative development of each individual.

SUMMARY

Careful consideration must be given to methods of presentation. Each aspect of the dance experience must be presented in a meaningful fashion. Various methods should be used and related in an appropriate manner so that the student will associate himself personally and receive full benefit of the presentation.

Evaluation should be included in the overall design as an integral part of the learning experience. Day-to-day evaluation by the teacher and students can give direction to the total experience and help to keep it meaningful and rewarding.

Bibliography

Anderson, Harold H. *Creativity and its Cultivation*. NY: Harper & Row, 1959.

Arnheim, Rudolf. *Art and Visual Perception*. Berkeley, CA: University of California Press, 1960.

Cohen, Selma Jeanne. *The Modern Dance: Seven Statements of Belief*. Middletown, CT: Wesleyan University Press, 1965.

Copeland, Roger, and Marshall Cohen. *What is Dance?* NY: Oxford University Press, 1983.

Copland, Aaron. *Music and Imagination*. Cambridge, MA: Harvard University Press, 1952.

Dell, Cecily. *A Primer for Movement Description Using Effort Shape and Supplementary Concepts*. NY: Dance Notation Bureau Press, 1977.

Dewey, John. *Art as Experience*. NY: Capricorn Books, 1934.

Ghiselan, Brewster. *The Creative Process*. NY: The New American Library, 1960.

H'Doubler, Margaret N. *Dance, A Creative Art Experience*. Madison, WI: The University of Wisconsin Press, 1957.

Hayes, Elizabeth R. *Dance Composition and Production*. Princeton, NJ: Dance Horizons/Princeton Book Co., Publishers, 1981.

Humphrey, Doris. *The Art of Making Dances*. NY: Holt, Rinehart, and Winston, 1959.

Jenkins, Iredell. *Art and The Human Enterprise*. Cambridge, MA: Harvard University Press, 1958.

Langer, Suzanne K. *Feeling and Form*. NY: Charles Scribner's Sons, 1953.

Livet, Ann. *Contemporary Dance*. NY: Abbeville Press, 1978.

Louis, Murray. *Inside Dance*. NY: St. Martin's Press, 1980.

Malraux, Andre. *The Voices of Silence*. NY: Doubleday and Co., 1953.

Martin, John. *The Modern Dance*. Princeton, NJ: Dance Horizons/Princeton Book Co., Publishers, 1965.

Martin, John. *Introduction to the Dance*. Princeton, NJ: Dance Horizons/Princeton Book Co., Publishers, 1965.

May, Rollo. *The Courage to Create*. NY: W. W. Norton and Co., 1975.

Metheny, Eleanor. *Body Dynamics*. NY: McGraw-Hill Book Co., 1952.

Murphy, Gardner. *Human Potentialities*. NY: Basic Books, 1958.

Rader, Melvin (ed.). *A Modern Book of Esthetics*. NY: Holt, Rinehart, and Winston, 1960.

Redfern, Betty. *Dance, Art and Aesthetics*. London: Dance Books Ltd., 1983.

Rogers, Frederick R. *Dance: A Basic Educational Technique*. Princeton, NJ: Dance Horizons/Princeton Book Co., Publishers, 1981.

Rugg, Harold. *Foundations for American Education*. NY: Harcourt, Brace and World, 1942.

Rugg, Harold. *Imagination*. NY: Harper & Row, 1963.

Schaeffer-Simmern, Henry. *Unfolding of Artistic Activity*. Berkeley, CA: University California Press, 1961.

Shahn, Ben. *The Shape of Content*. Cambridge, MA: Harvard University Press, 1960.

Smith, Jacqueline M. *Dance Composition*. London: A & C Black, 1986.

Smith, Paul. *Creativity*. NY: Hastings House, 1959.

Wigman, Mary. *The Language of Dance*. Middletown, CT: Wesleyan University Press, 1966.

Index

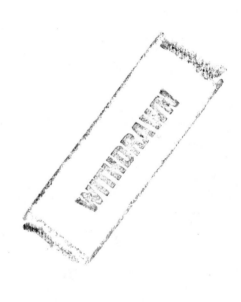